W9-BFX-038

BLUE GUIDE

Literary Companion

VENICE

Somerset Books • London

Blue Guide Literary Companion Venice
First edition 2009

Published by Blue Guides Limited, a Somerset Books Company
Winchester House, Deane Gate Avenue, Taunton, Somerset TA1 2UH
www.blueguides.com
'Blue Guide' is a registered trade mark

Maps by Dimap Bt., based on the maps in *Blue Guide Venice*
(8th edition)

ISBN 978-1-905131-32-7

A CIP catalogue record of this book is available from the British Library

Distributed in the United States of America by WW Norton and
Company, Inc. of 500 Fifth Avenue, New York, NY 10110

All Blue Guides are a collaborative endeavour. This book has been
assembled by Sophie Willats (editorial assistant) with contributions
from Thomas Howells (publisher), Charles Freeman (Blue Guides historical consultant), Nigel McGilchrist (Blue Guides art history and literature consultant) and Annabel Barber (editor-in-chief).
Layout by Anikó Kuzmich.
Details of contributors and their contributions are given on p. 224.

The Publisher wishes to thank Julia Bader, Jane Graham, Paul
Greatbatch, Kate Howells, George Starr and Michela Vanon Alliata.

CONTENTS

PREFACE

VENICE IN THEIR OWN WORDS

Travellers and visitors writing about 'abroad', poets and novelists who set their works there, generally aim to represent it realistically. More often than not, they end up telling posterity as much about themselves, their opinions, lives and interests, as about the destination. Writing about Venice is no exception. And although she has her own rich indigenous literature, this anthology concentrates largely on the writings of her 'literary' visitors, men and women of letters who have felt compelled to add to the vast body of foreigners' writings on Venice.

In medieval times Venice was one of Europe's most splendid, wealthy and powerful states. Visitors like Petrarch are suitably awed and respectful. Later on, by the 16th century, with the maturing of the Renaissance, prosperity coincided with a flourishing of the arts: the German painter Dürer visits, the Florentine art historian Vasari writes of Venice's great painters, architects and sculptors. By the 17th century the economic tide is slowly beginning to turn: visitors drawn by trade, curiosity and political intrigue, such as the ambassador-poet Henry Wotton or proto-adventure travel writer Thomas Coryate, are less awed and more inquisitive. By the 18th century Venice's music leads Europe, as J.J. Rousseau observes, but elsewhere the magnificence is wearing distinctly threadbare, and the whiff of decadence (which John Ruskin traces back to the curiously precise date of 1423) becomes a stench with Casanova's lurid tales of spying, gambling and seduction.

By the 19th century it was all over. The Most Serene Republic has fallen to Napoleon, who dissolved her institutions and destroyed her social fabric before handing her over to imperial Austria, in exchange for regions elsewhere. As a result she was an occupied territory for the first two thirds of the century. Poverty is widespread, and, deprived of independence or economic rationale, the humiliation of what had been one of Europe's greatest and richest powers is complete. 'Once did she hold the gorgeous East in fee' lamented Wordsworth in 1802. American and Victorian British poets and novelists, blithely assured of the 'moral and material' superiority of their home countries (the phrase belongs to William Dean Howells) were quick to join the chorus, relishing tales of vice and decrepitude, the inevitable wages of historical decadence.

Yet this was also the time of the birth of the Northern European and American dream of Italy. The young men of the Grand Tour had come to admire and study the works of Classical art. Inevitably they found themselves also philosophising amid the ruins, enjoying amorous encounters in alleyways, pouring out paeans of praise to a land where the sun shines and feelings are real. For Goethe in the 1780s or Byron in the 1820s Italy represented life as it should be lived, not the pale, hypocritical, rainy imitation to which the new middle classes of the industrial North were condemned. Soon the trend became a widely accepted fact: Italy was for life, love and laughter. Thus a dying Henry James heroine flies to Venice to experience a few last intense weeks; Dickens and Twain visit to generate exotic copy for home readers; and the painting and sculpture—the original, ostensible purpose of travel to Italy—is not forgotten either: wealthy collectors fed by Berenson's new art history buy Venetian old masters.

The resulting tourist trade slowly provided a recovery in Venice's fortunes. By the 20th century she had again become a glamorous destination, a backdrop for novels about life in *palazzi* by the likes of L.P. Hartley and Anthony Powell, and the subject of some of the best travel and history writing in the 20th century—for example by Jan Morris or John Julius Norwich—in itself literature about Venice.

In this anthology we include extracts from all of the above and more. The selection is by no means exhaustive, as the range of potential source material is huge. We should emphasise that the excerpts (ordered alphabetically) may be read or dipped into in whatever sequence suits the reader best. At the back of the book there is a thorough index, and the settings of the extracts are, where possible, shown on the maps at the front.

Thomas Howells, Publisher

Numbered dots on the maps show locations that relate to the extracts in the ensuing anthology. The names of authors of the extracts are shown in bold.

ST MARK'S SQUARE

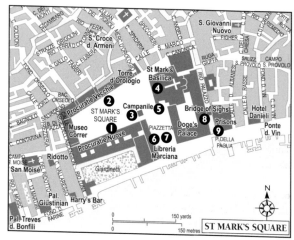

ST MARK'S SQUARE

1. Florian's

This famous café, where 'the immense cluster of tables and little chairs stretches like a promontory into the smooth lake of the Piazza', is the destination for the narrator on hot summer evenings in **Henry James**'s *The Aspern Papers* (1888; *see p. 120*). It is also where the journalist Merton Densher spies Lord Mark, his defeated rival for the dying Milly Theale's affections, on an afternoon of 'cold lashing rain' in James's *The Wings of the Dove* (1902; *see p. 123*).

2. St Mark's Square

Here litanies are decreed to be sung in 1513 to absolve the city of its sins and to ward off further earthquakes. The historian **Marin Sanudo** worries that they will not be effective, because earthquakes 'are a natural phenomenon' (*see p. 184*).

3. The Campanile of St Mark's

The poet **Goethe** first sees the Mediterranean sea from the top of the Campanile, the bell tower of St Mark's, in 1786.

4. St Mark's Basilica

On the balcony on the façade of St Mark's the poet **Petrarch** is given the place of honour beside the Doge to watch the celebrations in the square below of the Venetian re-capture of Crete in 1364. The spectators so pack the square that 'a grain of millet could not have fallen to earth' (*see p. 146*).

5. The Tetrarchs

These sculpted porphyry figures set into the southwest corner of St Mark's are traditionally believed to represent Roman emperors. **Thomas Coryate** sees them in 1608 and ascribes a more fanciful history to them (*see p. 61*).

6. The Libreria Marciana

The art historian **Giorgio Vasari** is fulsome in his praise for 'the beautiful and rich library opposite the public palace', designed by his fellow Tuscan, the architect Jacopo Sansovino, in 1537 (*see p. 200*).

7. The Piazzetta

Ezra Pound came here '*in my young youth / and lay there under the crocodile / By the column*', by which he meant the column of St Theodore, with his remarkably crocodile-like dragon, which stands between St Mark's Square and the water (*see p. 149*).

8. The Doge's Palace and 9. The Prisons

Casanova was imprisoned 'under the leads'—prison cells in the roof of the Doge's Palace—following his arrest in 1755 (*see p. 41*). Despite his libertinism and his gambling, it was for 'atheism' that he was convicted (probably one of the few offences that he did not commit), and he dramatically escapes by prising up one of the large lead roof tiles (*see p. 43*). There were also prison cells in the Palace's flood-prone cellars: **Samuel Rogers** in his lengthy 1828 poem *Italy* tells us melodramatically of the 'dripping vaults under the flood where light and warmth came never' which he contrasts with those under the roof where temperatures soared in the summer and 'reason flees' (*see p. 158*). These cells are connected to the prison proper by an arched, covered stone bridge, in the 19th century romantically named the 'Bridge of Sighs'. **John Ruskin** was unmoved by this imagery, prosaically opining in *The Stones of Venice* (1853): 'No prisoner, whose name is worth remembering, or whose sorrow deserved sympathy, ever crossed that 'Bridge of Sighs,' which is the centre of the Byronic ideal of Venice' (*see p. 179*).

VENICE WEST

10. Palazzo Vendramin-Calergi
Richard Wagner died here in 1883 following a heart attack. Some rooms serve as a small museum. The main part of the *palazzo* is now the Municipal Casino.

11. The Ghetto
In Venice's historic Jewish district, the eccentric traveller **Thomas Coryate** tried to convert a rabbi to Christianity and had to be rescued from an angry crowd by the poet-ambassador **Sir Henry Wotton**'s gondola in 1608.

12. Santa Lucia railway station
Where **William Dean Howells** arrives for the first time on a freezing 'ink-black' night in 1861 (*see p. 114*).

13. Palazzo Soranzo-Cappello
The model for the faded mansion with a rambling garden described by **Henry James** in *The Aspern Papers* (1888; *see p. 120*).

14. Fondaco dei Tedeschi

Albrecht Dürer lived here on his first visit to Venice in 1494, before the building burnt down and its replacement was frescoed by Giorgione and Titian (*see* **Ezra Pound**'s *Canto XXV; p. 148*).

15. The Rialto Bridge

In his poem *A Toccata of Galuppi's* (1855; *see p. 30*) **Robert Browning** writes of the bridge: '*Ay, because the sea's the street there, and 'tis arched by…what you call / …Shylock's bridge with houses on it, where they kept the carnival.*'

16. At Monsieur Marzari's near the Rialto

One evening in January 1850 **Effie Ruskin** leaves her husband **John** working on *The Stones of Venice* to attend Monsieur Marzari's party. She is impressed, remarking that 'I never saw such good-breeding, almost amounting to severity & prudery' (*see p. 174*).

17. Palazzo Mocenigo

Where **Lord Byron** lived with his menagerie of two mastiffs, two monkeys, and a fox.

18. Ca' Rezzonico

This *palazzo* facing the Grand Canal was bought by Fanny and Pen Browning in 1888. Pen's father, the poet **Robert Browning**, died here after catching a chill on a visit a year later. (*And see J.G. Links on p. 127 for the difference, or lack of one, between a* palazzo *and a* ca'.)

19. Ponte dei Pugni

A bridge without parapets, where fights were staged between pugilists from rival *sestieri*, as described by **Hugh A. Douglas** in his 1907 *Venice on Foot* (*see p. 75*). After one fight ended in a bloody battle between the spectators in 1705 the practice was banned.

20. The Accademia Bridge

In his *Venice for Pleasure*, **J.G. Links** stands on the bridge looking

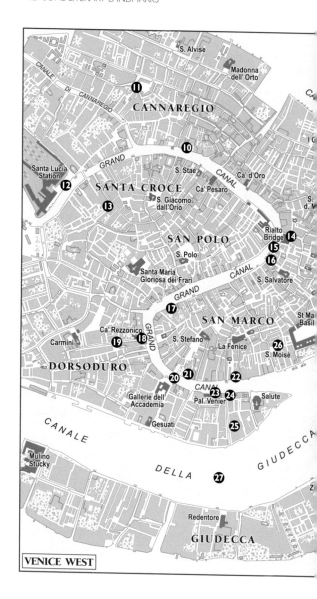

VENICE WEST

0

500 yards

0

500 metres

N

33 ISOLA
DI SAN MICHELE

FONDAMENTE NUOVE

ovanni e Paolo

S. Francesco
d. Vigna

Formosa

CASTELLO

28

DARSENA
GRANDE

S. Pietro
in Castello

Zaccaria

S. Giovanni
in Bragora

Arsenale

ISOLA DI
SAN PIETRO

29

2

San Giorgio
Maggiore

ISOLA DI
S. GIORGIO
MAGGIORE

CANALE DI SAN MARCO

31 Biennale

ISOLA DI
S. ELENA

VENICE EAST

up the Grand Canal to Browning's Ca' Rezzonico and down as far as the Salute (*see p. 126*).

21. Palazzo Barbaro

Henry James writes much of *The Aspern Papers* (1888; *see p. 120*) here. He also makes it Milly Theale's rented 'Palazzo Leporelli' in *The Wings of the Dove* (1902; *see p. 123*).

22. The Gritti Palace Hotel

Formerly the Palazzo Wetzler where **John** and **Effie Ruskin** rent an apartment on their second stay in 1851–52.

23. Palazzo Venier dei Leoni

The unfinished *palazzo* on the Grand Canal that was **Peggy Guggenheim**'s house is now a museum, part of the Solomon R. Guggenheim Foundation. There is a small collection of good examples from the major art movements of the first half of the 20th century, but the star remains Peggy herself (*see p. 94*).

24. Casa Semitecolo

'Miss Woolson's sad death-house', in the words of **Henry James**. From an upper window the novelist Constance Fenimore Woolson falls to her death on a winter's night in 1894 (*see p. 120*).

25. Calle Querini

Ezra Pound lived here on and off for much of his life, in a small house at no. 252, with his partner Olga Rudge. Translated, the plaque on the wall reads: '*In his undying love for Venice, Ezra Pound, titan of poetry, lived in this house for half a century*'.

26. The church of San Moisè

William Dean Howells attends Midnight Mass here one Christmas Eve in the 1860s and does not like the architecture (*see p. 117*). Like many subsequent visitors he adopts Ruskin's views on aesthetics, roundly condemning in particular the Baroque. Forty years earlier **Lord Byron** rented rooms over a draper's shop by San Moisè. He narrates at length an incident in his affair with the draper's wife during the carnival of 1817 in a letter to his friend, and subsequent editor of his letters, Thomas Moore (*see p. 34*).

27. The Giudecca Canal

Mark Twain 'never enjoyed [himself] better' than when singing songs from a gondola here, on the occasion of the 1867 Feast of the Redentore. The feast is still held every year on the third Sunday in July, when a bridge of boats is assembled from the Zattere to Palladio's church of the Redentore (*see p. 193*).

VENICE EAST

28. Scuola di San Giorgio degli Schiavoni

'Piquantly charming' according to **Jan Morris**. The scuola is filled with paintings by Carpaccio, its 'four walls positively smile with the genius of this delightful painter' (*see p. 140*).

29. Riva degli Schiavoni

The broad quay where in 1508 **Albrecht Dürer** finds that the 'falsest knaves' were selling everything for four times what it was worth, and it was all bought up by the Germans (*see p. 78*).

30. The Hotel Danieli

Named after its Swiss founder, Joseph dal Niel, who opened it as a hotel in 1822. Guests have included: **Effie** and **John Ruskin** in 1849–50, **Dickens** in 1846, **Wagner**, and **Proust** in 1900.

31. The Paradiso restaurant at the Biennale Park

When war prevents the Greeks from occupying their national pavilion in 1948, **Peggy Guggenheim** takes it over to display her ground-breaking collection of modern art. While she attends to hanging the exhibition, her dogs are 'very well treated' and fed ice cream at the restaurant (*see p. 97*).

32. The Island of San Giorgio Maggiore

The industrialist Vittorio Cini took a lease on the island after the Second World War to provide a home for some of his collection and for his charitable works, which included educating orphans and sailors' children. His foundation also organises international conferences. The fictional publisher Nicholas Jenkins, narrator of **Anthony Powell**'s twelve-volume *Dance to the Music of Time*, attends such a conference here in the 1950s (*see p. 152*).

33. The Island of San Michele

Venice's cemetery. The modernist poet **Ezra Pound** is buried here, as is **Baron Corvo (Frederick Rolfe),** who lies in the Catholic part of the cemetery. Although he had been dismissed from the seminary he attended in Rome, he persisted in styling himself 'Fr. Rolfe' to give the impression he was 'Father' Rolfe (*see p. 54*).

THE LAGOON

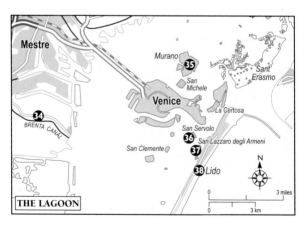

34. The Brenta Canal

Travelling alongside the canal from the city of Padua to Venice in the 1750s, **Casanova** runs to the aid of a certain Signorina C.

when her carriage overturns. His good deed leads to one of his numerous love affairs (*see p. 38*).

35. Murano

Famous since the 13th century for its glass manufacture, **James Howell** visits between 1616 and 1619 to get ideas for his glass-works in London (*see p. 109*). **J.J. Rousseau**'s delightful companion, Zulietta, takes him to Murano in 1745 so that he can buy her glass baubles. Alas, his efforts to win her approval fail and she dismisses him with a put-down he would never forget, namely that he should forget about women and stick to his studies (*see p. 164*).

36. The Island of San Servolo

Eustace, the protagonist in **L.P. Hartley**'s 1944 novel *Eustace and Hilda*, sails past this island, then serving as a lunatic asylum, on his dawn return from the Lido. He hopes he will be able to contain his seasickness in front of the Venetian family whose boat he shares (*see p. 101*).

37. The Island of San Lazzaro

During his stay in Venice in 1816–21 **Byron** would retire to this island, home to Armenian monks, to study their language.

38. The Lido

On arriving in Venice, Aschenbach, the protagonist of **Thomas Mann**'s 1912 novella *Death in Venice* (*see p. 128*) is left bemused at the Lido landing stage when his unlicensed gondolier flees without payment. **Byron** kept a horse on the Lido and used to gallop up and down its sands in search of 'conspicuous solitude' in **W.D. Howells**'s words. Byron was born with a lame foot, and riding and swimming were two ways he could prove his strength. On one occasion he swims all the way from the Lido to the northern end of the Grand Canal in three and three quarter hours.

PIETRO BEMBO

Venetian by birth, Pietro Bembo (1470–1547) was brought up and educated in various Italian cities including Florence, where his father served as Venetian ambassador. As a result he was able to absorb the cultural and intellectual attitudes of the Renaissance through its leading proponents, especially those in the circle of Lorenzo the Magnificent. Bembo particularly revered the poet Petrarch (see p. 143), believing that the latter's Tuscan Italian represented an ideal to which all scholars should aspire. He also mastered Greek, which for Florentine scholars was an essential accoutrement of the cultivated intellectual. Bembo travelled widely in Italy. He was for a time at Ferrara, where he met Lucrezia Borgia, to whom he dedicated his famous discourse on Platonic love, Gli Asolani. Byron was to call the correspondence between them the 'prettiest love letters in the world'. Bembo also formed part of the court circle of the Duke of Urbino (he is one of the speakers in Castiglione's famous treatise on manners, The Courtier, *set in Urbino in 1508). With the accession to the papacy of Lorenzo the Magnificent's son, as Pope Leo X, Bembo was summoned to Rome as papal secretary. His career in the Church did not prevent him becoming the father of three children by one Moresina, the love of his life.*

Despite his travels, Bembo remained at the centre of Venetian scholarship and has been seen as one of those who replaced the traditional Venetian focus on business with literary and cultural ideals. He enjoyed a close relationship with the famous printer Aldus Manutius, who had moved to Venice in 1490 and produced the first high-quality editions of many of the Greek classics. In his villa near Padua, Bembo accumulated a wonderful collection of art, which included works by the Venetian painters Mantegna and Giovanni Bellini as well as Raphael, a native of Urbino and favourite artist of Leo X.

In 1529 Bembo was appointed the official historian for Venice (fellow historian Marin Sanudo, see p. 182, was disappointed to be passed over) and completed the volumes for the years 1487 to 1513. He proved a fine stylist and his wide experience of the other city states of Italy allowed him to discuss Venice's foreign policy with authority. In his final years Bembo returned to Rome to enjoy the papal patronage of Paul III, who made him a cardinal. He died in the city.

Bembo's History of Venice *was published after his death, in 1551. It gives a fascinating insight into the concerns of the Republic's rulers.*

History of Venice (1551)
Pietro Bembo

At that time too [1489], the Senate passed a law to give more generous treatment to the illegitimate children who were raised at public expense and whose numbers had greatly increased, by having the Officers of the Arsenal make their keepers an annual grant of 200 bushels (as they call them) of wheat and twelve casks of wine, and by having their superintendents add on top of that 200 cartloads of timber for firewood from the Republic's stores. Not long afterwards, the city was thrown into panic when on 11th August the two greatest and tallest towers in the city, one in St. Mark's Square whose roof was gilded and the other in the middle of the city at the church of the Friars Minor [the Frari], were struck by lightning at night and caught fire, the blaze that consumed their roofs visible far and wide. Following that, the Senate gave its attention to promulgating various laws directed at maintaining the city's revenue from tariffs. Also, on the last day of the year, nuns were brought into the church of Santa Maria, famous for the miracles from which it takes its name [Santa Maria dei Miracoli]: the building was now finished with workmanship all the more splendid for its being so small, so that the beauty and richness of its materials equalled the grandeur of other churches.

…another law which greatly benefited the city was brought before the Great Council by the councillor Antonio Tron. His law on casting votes soon put an end to abuses in the election of magistrates, which had become by now intolerable. The system of voting in place up to that time was as follows: with the citizens seated on benches, two boxes of turned wood, each a foot high, were brought in, one green, the other white. The upper part of the boxes was open and they spread out so that a hand could be put in, while in the middle they contracted to a narrow passage so that only a single ballot could get further inside, while also making it much handier to pick up and carry around. The bottom could hold a great many votes, and could be removed and replaced, as it was when the votes were counted. Each voter would cast his ballot into his preferred urn. The ballot itself was a little ball the size of a small cherry and made of cloth, not hard and solid, but loosely sewn together so as to make it impossible to hear into which urn the ball had fallen. By law the voters would put their hands into both urns with fist clenched, again to make it impossible to know in which urn the ballot had been left. The balls that were cast into the white urn represented votes for the candidate, those in the green one votes against.

Although this system had been set up long before electoral fraud (to which every republic in history has obviously been exposed) had become so outrageous that someone who favored the election of one of his followers would take the ball in his fingers and openly cast it into the white urn, and demand that those around him should do the same. They in turn would fear the resentment of the candidates, and would cast their vote in full view, not usually following their own judgment but in order to curry favour. And so it came about that men who were not worthy of it were often preferred to citizens who had served the Republic well, simply because they had greater influence thanks to their wealth or family or patronage in general. They won the magistracies while good men were spurned and rejected.

Numerous laws in the past had done nothing to counter this pernicious evil and eradicate it from civic life. It was only with the passing of Antonio Tron's legislation that integrity and honor were restored to the citizens. His plan was that the two urns, which it had hitherto been customary to have carried around open and uncovered by civil servants, should be covered in their upper part and joined together side by side. He made a single opening in the

urns thus connected and welded together, towards the side of the
top covering, and around it he put a projecting cuff the width of
half a palm, so obscuring the openings to the insides of the boxes.
Through this tube a hand could be inserted and easily turned
towards either of the boxes. Another feature was that the first of
the two urns, the one placed next to the cuff; was the one whose
balls rejected candidates. By this device Tron intended that if a
man was compelled to vote for someone against his will, he could
secretly open his fingers and drop the ballot in the near compart-
ment as he extended his hand through the mouth of the tube
towards the far one, the one whose votes elected a magistrate. In
this way the citizens could pretend to do one thing and not the
other and so actually bring about what each of them wanted, nor
could what they had done be detected or discovered. Thenceforth
the citizenry always used this procedure in the Great Council and
in appointing magistrates in the Senate and the Council of Ten,
its decisions free of favor or spite. In capital cases and all other
judicial proceedings, however, they brought in an additional third
urn, so that if someone was undecided, he might place his vote
there. They resolved to keep this urn separate and unconnected
to the other two.

Reprinted by permission of the publisher from Pietro Bembo, History of
Venice: Vol. 1, *edited and translated by Robert W Ulery, The I Tatti Renaissance Library Volume 28, pp. 55; 59–61; 67–71, Cambridge, Mass.:
Harvard University Press, Copyright © 2007 by the President and Fellows
of Harvard College.*

BERNARD BERENSON

Born in Lithuania, the son of parents who emigrated to Boston, Massachusetts, Bernard Berenson (1865–1959) was America's most influential art historian and critic in the first half of the 20th century. When he graduated from Harvard, the Boston collector Isabella Stewart Gardner supported his travels in Europe, where he went to develop his planned career as a novelist. In Oxford he was influenced by the leading Renaissance scholars of the day, and at the age of 35, financed by scouting for the major galleries, by arts dealings on his own behalf and by the success of his writings on Italian Renaissance art (see below), he bought the Villa I Tatti outside Florence, where he was to live for most of the remaining 60 years of his life. Now serving as the Harvard University Center for Italian Renaissance Studies, it was to be his most lasting monument.

His now unfashionably elitist doctrine of 'connoisseurship' (see below) and the fact that he was deeply compromised in his commercial relationships with dealers—he often received enormous undisclosed commissions from sellers and dealers as a result of authenticating works for the purchaser—have combined to obscure the brilliance of his writing on Italian painting and the extraordinary influence it had on subsequent art history.

*He wrote one of the first of his books on Italian painting—*Venetian Painters of the Renaissance—*in 1894.* Florentine *(1896),* Central Italian *(1897) and* North Italian Painters of the Renaissance *(1907) followed. These were collected into* The Italian Painters of the Renaissance *in 1930 which sold worldwide in many editions and languages. Berenson's 'scientific connoisseurship' combined technical analysis of minutiae—the detail of how a garment's fabric or a hand were rendered, for example—with a belief in the almost religious benefits—of bliss and release—to be derived from contemplation of great art, preferably harmonious Renaissance art, for its own sake. The former was important for the attribution of paintings, which was the main purpose of art history in the late 19th century, the latter dominated it for much of the 20th.*

Venetian Painters of the Renaissance (1894)
Bernard Berenson

Among the Italian schools of painting the Venetian has, for the majority of art-loving people, the strongest and most enduring attraction. In the course of the present brief account of the life of that school we shall perhaps discover some of the causes of our peculiar delight and interest in the Venetian painters, as we come to realise what tendencies of the human spirit their art embodied, and of what great consequence their example has been to the whole of European painting for the last three centuries.

The Venetians as a school were from the first endowed with exquisite tact in their use of colour. Seldom cold and rarely too warm, their colouring never seems an afterthought, as in many of the Florentine painters, nor is it always suggesting paint, as in some of the Veronese masters. When the eye has grown accustomed to make allowance for the darkening caused by time, for the dirt that lies in layers on so many pictures, and for unsuccessful attempts at restoration, the better Venetian paintings present such harmony of intention and execution as distinguishes the highest achievements of genuine poets. Their mastery over colour is the first thing that attracts most people to the painters of Venice. Their colouring not only gives direct pleasure to the eye, but acts like music upon the moods, stimulating thought and memory in much the same way as a work by a great composer.

…Painting had in his [Giovanni Bellini's] lifetime reached a point where the difficulties of technique no longer stood in the way of the expression of profound emotion. No one can look at Bellini's pictures of the Dead Christ upheld by the Virgin or angels without being put into a mood of deep contrition, nor at his earlier Madonnas without a thrill of awe and reverence. And Giovanni Bellini does not stand alone. His contemporaries, Gentile Bellini, the Vivarini, Crivelli, and Cima da Conegliano all began by painting in the same spirit, and produced almost the same effect.

…At about the time when Bellini and his contemporaries were

attaining maturity, the Renaissance had ceased to be a movement carried on by scholars and poets alone. It had become sufficiently widespread to seek popular as well as literary utterance, and thus, toward the end of the fifteenth century, it naturally turned to painting, a vehicle of expression which the Church, after a thousand years of use, had made familiar and beloved.

When it once reached the point where its view of the world naturally sought expression in painting, as religious ideas had done before, the Renaissance found in Venice clearer utterance than elsewhere, and it is perhaps this fact which makes the most abiding interest of Venetian painting. It is at this point that we shall take it up.

The growing delight in life with the consequent love of health, beauty, and joy were felt more powerfully in Venice than anywhere else in Italy. The explanation of this may be found in the character of the Venetian government which was such that it gave little room for the satisfaction of the passion for personal glory, and kept its citizens so busy in duties of state that they had small leisure for learning. Some of the chief passions of the Renaissance thus finding no outlet in Venice, the other passions insisted all the more on being satisfied. Venice, moreover, was the only state in Italy which was enjoying, and for many generations had been enjoying, internal peace. This gave the Venetians a love of comfort, of ease, and of splendour, a refinement of manner, and humaneness of feeling, which made them the first really modern people in Europe. Since there was little room for personal glory in Venice, the perpetuators of glory, the Humanists, found at first scant encouragement there, and the Venetians were saved from that absorption in archæology and pure science which overwhelmed Florence at an early date. This was not necessarily an advantage in itself, but it happened to suit Venice, where the conditions of life had for some time been such as to build up a love of beautiful things. As it was, the feeling for beauty was not hindered in its natural development. Archæology would have tried to submit it to the good taste of the past, a proceeding which rarely promotes good taste in the present. Too much archæology and too much science might have ended in making Venetian art academic, instead of letting it become what it did, the product of a natural ripening of interest in life and love of pleasure. In Florence, it is true, painting had developed almost simultaneously with the other arts, and it may be due to this very cause that the Florentine painters never quite realised what a different task from the architect's and sculptor's was theirs. At the time, therefore, when the Renaissance was beginning to find its best expression in painting, the Florentines were already too much attached to classical ideals of form and composition, in other words, too academic, to give embodiment to the throbbing feeling for life and pleasure.

Thus it came to pass that in the Venetian pictures of the end of the fifteenth century we find neither the contrition nor the devotion of those earlier years when the Church alone employed painting as the interpreter of emotion, nor the learning which characterised the Florentines. The Venetian masters of this time, although nominally continuing to paint the Madonna and saints, were in reality painting handsome, healthy, sane people like themselves, people who wore their splendid robes with dignity, who found life worth the mere living and sought no metaphysical basis for it. In short, the Venetian pictures of the last decade of the century seemed intended not for devotion, as they had been, nor for admiration, as they then were in Florence, but for enjoyment.

Venetian Painters of the Renaissance, *Bernard Berenson, 3rd edition, G.P. Putnam's Sons, 1894.*

ELIZABETH BARRETT BROWNING

Elizabeth Barrett Moulton Barrett (1806–61) was a successful poet long before her marriage to Robert Browning (see p. 29) at the age of 38 (the double Barrett was her father's strategy to prevent the Barrett name being lost should his daughters marry—an eventuality he did everything in his power to prevent). Largely self-taught, she envied her brother's opportunities for education, and while he was at school she stayed at home avidly reading anything she could lay her hands on, which included Homer and Virgil in the original. At the age of 14 she published an epic on the Battle of Marathon and at 21 a long Byronic poem, The Development of Genius.

Ill-health kept her at home for much of the time and many of her friendships—including her initial one with Browning—were conducted entirely or largely by correspondence. Later friends included Samuel Rogers (q.v.), John Ruskin (q.v.) and Thackeray. It was her father's expected opposition to her marriage and subsequent disinheritance of Elizabeth that caused her and Browning to remove to Italy; first Pisa, then Florence. Their financial independence was achieved by a legacy from an uncle. During her lifetime, Elizabeth's reputation stood much higher than her husband's. She was considered a competitor of Tennyson for the post of Poet Laureate in 1850.

In 1857 she wrote the lengthy poem Aurora Leigh, *which Ruskin called the 'greatest poem of the century'. Later hailed as 'feminist', it portrayed the life of a female artist, addressing issues of class and women's rights. Though it polarised opinion, it was a literary success, particularly in America, where it sold well and continued to do so for several decades after her death.*

Elizabeth Barrett Browning did not spend much time in Venice, visiting only in 1851 with Robert and her maid Wilson, accompanied by their spaniel, Flush. Here are two descriptions from her letters, the first to the writer Mary Russell Mitford, the second to John Kenyon, a distant cousin on her father's side. It is interesting to note that despite

Robert's latter strong association with Venice, it was clearly not love at first sight, and on this early visit Elizabeth clearly enjoys herself while Robert is unable to eat or sleep.

Letters (1851–61)
Elizabeth Barrett Browning

To Miss Mitford

4th June [1851]

I have been between heaven and earth since our arrival at Venice. The heaven of it is ineffable. Never had I touched the skirts of so celestial a place. The beauty of the architecture, the silver trails of water up between all that gorgeous colour and carving, the enchanting silence, the moonlight, the music, the gondolas—I mix it all up together, and maintain that nothing is like it, nothing equal to it, not a second Venice in the world. Do you know, when I came first I felt as if I never could go away. But now comes the earth side. Robert, after sharing the ecstasy, grows uncomfortable, and nervous, and unable to eat or sleep; and poor Wilson, still worse, in a miserable condition of continual sickness and headache. Alas for these mortal Venices—so exquisite and so bilious! Therefore I am constrained away from my joys by sympathy, and am forced to be glad that we are going off on Friday. For myself, it does not affect me at all. I like these moist, soft, relaxing climates; even the scirocco doesn't touch me much. And the baby grows gloriously fatter in spite of everything.

To Mr Kenyon

7th July [1851]

Venice is quite exquisite; it wrapt me round with a spell at first sight, and I longed to live and die there—never to go away. The gondolas, and the glory they swim through, and the silence of the population, drifted over one's head across the bridges, and the fantastic architecture and the coffee-drinking and music in the Piazza San Marco, everything fitted into my lazy, idle nature and weakness of body, as if I had been born to the manner of it and to no other. Do you know I expected in Venice a dreary sort of desolation? Whereas there was nothing melancholy at all, only a soothing, lulling, rocking atmosphere which if Armida had lived in a city rather than in a garden would have suited her purpose. Indeed Taglioni seems to be resting her feet from dancing, there, with a peculiar zest, inasmuch as she has bought three or four of the most beautiful palaces. How could she do better? And one or two ex-kings and queens (of the more vulgar royalties) have wrapt themselves round with those shining waters to forget the purple—or dream of it, as the case may be. Robert and I led a true Venetian life, I assure you; we 'swam in gondolas' to the Lido and everywhere else, we went to a festa at Chioggia in the steamer (frightening Wilson by being kept out by the wind till two o'clock in the morning), we went to the opera and the play (at a shilling each, or not as much!), and we took coffee every evening on St. Mark's Piazza, to music and the stars. Altogether it would have been perfect, only what's perfect in the world? While I grew fat, Wilson grew thin, and Robert could not sleep at nights. The air was too relaxing or soft or something for them both, and poor Wilson declares that another month of Venice would have killed her outright. Certainly she looked dreadfully ill and could eat nothing. So I was forced to be glad to go away, out of pure humanity and sympathy, though I keep saying softly to myself ever since, 'What is there on earth like Venice?'.

The Letters of Elizabeth Barrett Browning, *Elizabeth Barrett Browning, Smith, Elder & Co., 1897. Reproduced by permission of the Provost and Fellows of Eton College.*

ROBERT BROWNING

Robert Browning (1812–89) began his literary life—in dress and style of poetry at least—as a foppish imitator of Shelley and Byron. Unlike Byron, however, he had no fortune to dissipate and his private life and views—except maybe his occasional assaults on organised religion— were generally respectable and thoroughly 'Victorian'. Many of his earlier poems were long and obscure. He based the 5,800-line poem Sordello *on assumed reader knowledge of Guelph and Ghibelline struggles in medieval Tuscany with very little explanation. Everyone was baffled—except Ezra Pound (q.v.), who based many of his own poems on obscure snatches from Italian history and 70 years later described* Sordello *as 'a model of lucidity'. By the time of his death in Venice in 1889, however, Browning had risen to a place of affection in the public's heart, considered a Grand Old Man of Literature, with dozens of 'Browning Societies' throughout the English-speaking world.*

Browning's great talent was for poetry as drama, and in Italy, with its colourful cast of characters, he found a rich seam to mine. He was well qualified to write about the country: immediately after marrying the poet Elizabeth Barrett (q.v.) in 1846, he fled with her to Pisa and thence to Florence. Elizabeth died in 1861 and Browning returned to England, but from 1878 on he spent several months a year in Venice. In later years he stayed in the Ca' Rezzonico on the Grand Canal (the apartment where he lived and died is open to the public), which Pen Browning—his and Elizabeth's only child—and Pen's wealthy American wife Fanny Coddington bought and splendidly refurbished. Browning died in Ca' Rezzonico on 12th December 1889.

Browning is known today chiefly for his shorter poems, notably his dramatic monologues or for lyrics inspired by his other great love, music. The poem quoted below comes from the collection Men and Women, *published in 1855 and dedicated to his wife. A toccata is a musical composition designed to show off a pianist's technical skills; Baldassare Galuppi (1706–84) was a Venetian composer from the island of Burano who, amongst other works, co-wrote popular comic operas with Carlo Goldoni. Galuppi visited England in 1741 to write opera for the Haymarket Theatre. Browning is known to have owned manuscripts of Galuppi's compositions.*

A Toccata of Galuppi's (1855)
Robert Browning

Oh Galuppi, Baldassaro, this is very sad to find!
I can hardly misconceive you; it would prove me deaf and blind;
But although I give you credit, 'tis with such a heavy mind!

Here you come with your old music, and here's all the good it
    brings.
What, they lived once thus at Venice, where the merchants were
    the kings,
Where St. Mark's is, where the Doges used to wed the sea with
    rings?

Ay, because the sea's the street there, and 'tis arched by…what
    you call
…Shylock's bridge with houses on it, where they kept the
    carnival:
I was never out of England—it's as if I saw it all.

Did young people take their pleasure when the sea was warm in
    May?
Balls and masks begun at midnight, burning ever to mid-day,
When they made up fresh adventures for the morrow, do you
    say?
Was a lady such a lady, cheeks so round and lips so red,—
On her neck the small face buoyant, like a bell-flower on its bed,

O'er the breast's superb abundance where a man might base his
   head?

Well (and it was graceful of them) they'd break talk off and af-
   ford
—She, to bite her mask's black velvet he, to finger on his sword,
While you sat and played Toccatas, stately at the clavichord?

What? Those lesser thirds so plaintive, sixths diminished, sigh
   on sigh,
Told them something? Those suspensions, those solutions 'Must
   we die?'
Those commiserating sevenths—'Life might last! we can but try!'

'Were you happy?'—'Yes.'—'And are you still as happy?'
'Yes—And you?'
—'Then more kisses'—'Did I stop them, when a million seemed
   so few?'
Hark—the dominant's persistence, till it must be answered to!

So, an octave struck the answer. Oh, they praised you, I dare
   say!
'Brave Galuppi! that was music! good alike at grave and gay!
I can always leave off talking when I hear a master play!'

Then they left you for their pleasure: till in due time, one by
   one,
Some with lives that came to nothing, some with deeds as well
   undone,
Death came tacitly and took them where they never see the sun.

But when I sit down to reason,—think to take my stand nor
   swerve,
While I triumph o'er a secret wrung from nature's close reserve,
In you come with your cold music, till I creep thro' every nerve.

Yes, you, like a ghostly cricket, creaking where a house was
    burned—
'Dust and ashes, dead and done with, Venice spent what Venice
    earned!
The soul, doubtless, is immortal—where a soul can be dis-
    cerned.

'Yours for instance, you know physics, something of geology,
Mathematics are your pastime; souls shall rise in their degree;
Butterflies may dread extinction,—you'll not die, it cannot be!

'As for Venice and its people, merely born to bloom and drop,
Here on earth they bore their fruitage, mirth and folly were the
    crop.
What of soul was left, I wonder, when the kissing had to stop?

'Dust and ashes!' So you creak it, and I want the heart to scold.
Dear dead women, with such hair, too—what's become of all the
    gold
Used to hang and brush their bosoms? I feel chilly and grown
    old.

Originally published in the poetry collection Men and Women, *Robert Browning, Chapman & Hall, 1855. Reproduced by permission of the Provost and Fellows of Eton College.*

LORD BYRON

George Gordon Byron (1788–1824) was the most-read poet of his generation. And though his poetry has not aged well—his rambling, mock-epic poems such as Childe Harold's Pilgrimage (1812–17) and Don Juan (1818–20) are seldom read in their entirety—it was never for his poetry alone that Byron was known; his scandalous private life was as much a subject for celebrity gossip two hundred years ago as it would be now.

Etching from the book *Portrait Gallery of Eminent Men and Women in Europe and America*, published in 1873.

After his highly-publicised flight from the amorous attentions of Lady Caroline Lamb, he married the brilliant mathematician Anne Isabella Milbanke, who left him in 1816 claiming he was insane. He promptly departed London and set off for Venice—'the greenest island of my imagination' he wrote to his friend and fellow poet Thomas Moore—pausing briefly on the way in Ostende 'to fall upon the chambermaid like a thunderbolt' according to his physician, and in Geneva to sail on the lake with his friend, the poet Shelley. After his arrival in Venice he rented rooms above a draper's shop near San Moisè from a Signor Segati, before moving to the Palazzo Mocenigo on the Grand Canal with his menagerie of monkeys, dogs and a fox. During his time in Venice he not only 'abandoned himself to degrading excesses' (according to the Concise Dictionary of National Biography), he also studied Armenian from the monks of San Lazzaro (he fell out with them when they did not use the introduction he wrote for an Armenian and English Grammar) and would gallop the horses he kept on the Lido up and down the Adriatic shore 'in search of that conspicuous solitude of which the sincere bard was fond', as William Dean Howells (q.v.) dryly remarked some 40 years later. On one occasion he swam back from the Lido to the north end of the Grand Canal in three and three quarter hours, relishing not only the fact that he

*alone among his companions successfully completed the challenge, but
also the company of the 'piece' he enjoyed on his return to the Palazzo
Mocenigo, proving that he was not in the least fatigued.*

*He left Venice for the last time in 1821 and stayed with Shelley and
his wife Mary in Pisa, until Shelley's tragic death in a boating accident.
After journeys to Genoa and Cephalonia, restless by nature and in ill
health from debauchery, Byron died in 1824 of malaria at Missolonghi
in mainland Greece, where he had gone to raise an army to fight for the
cause of Greek independence from the Turks.*

*In the following letter to Thomas Moore, Byron describes an incident
in his affair with Marianna Segati—'in appearance altogether like an
antelope'—the wife of his first landlord in Venice.*

Letters and Journals (1817)
Lord Byron

To Thomas Moore

28th January 1817

…Venice is in the *estro* of her carnival, and I have been up these
last two nights at the ridotto and the opera, and all that kind of
thing. Now for an adventure.

A few days ago a gondolier brought me a billet without a sub-
scription, intimating a wish on the part of the writer to meet me
either in gondola or at the island of San Lazaro [sic.], or at a third
rendezvous, indicated in the note. 'I know the country's disposition well'—in Venice 'they do let Heaven see those tricks they
dare not show,' &c. &c.; so, for all response, I said that neither of
the three places suited me; but that I would either be at home at
ten at night *alone*, or at the ridotto at midnight, where the writer
might meet me masked. At ten o'clock I was at home and alone
(Marianna was gone with her husband to a *conversazione*), when
the door of my apartment opened, and in walked a well-looking
and (for an Italian) *bionda* girl of about nineteen, who informed

me that she was married to the brother of my *amorosa* [Marianna], and wished to have some conversation with me. I made a decent reply, and we had some talk in Italian and Romaic (her mother being a Greek of Corfu), when lo! in a very few minutes, in marches, to my very great astonishment, Marianna S, *in propria persona*, and after making polite courtesy to her sister-in-law and to me, without a single word seizes her said sister-in-law by the hair, and bestows upon her some sixteen slaps, which would have made your ear ache only to hear their echo. I need not describe the screaming which ensued. The luckless visitor took flight. I seized Marianna, who, after several vain efforts to get away in pursuit of the enemy, fairly went into fits in my arms; and, in spite of reasoning, eau de Cologne, vinegar, half a pint of water, and God knows what other waters beside, continued so till past midnight.

After damning my servants for letting people in without apprizing me, I found that Marianna in the morning had seen her sister-in-law's gondolier on the stairs, and, suspecting that his apparition boded her no good, had either returned of her own accord, or been followed by her maids or some other spy of her people to the *conversazione*, from whence she returned to perpetrate this piece of pugilism. I had seen fits before, and also some small scenery of the same genus in and out of our island: but this was not all. After about an hour, in comes who? Why, Signor S, her lord and husband, and finds me with his wife fainting upon the sofa, and all the apparatus of confusion, dishevelled hair, hats, handkerchiefs, salts, smelling-bottles—and the lady as pale as ashes without sense or motion. His first question was, 'What is all this?' The lady could not reply—so I did. I told him the explanation was the easiest thing in the world; but in the mean time it would be as well to recover his wife—at least, her senses. This came about in due time of suspiration and respiration. You need not be alarmed—jealousy is not the order of the day in Venice, and daggers are out of fashion; while duels, on love matters, are unknown—at least, with the husbands. But, for all this, it was an awkward affair; and though he must have known that I made love to Marianna, yet I believe he was not, till that evening, aware of the extent to which it had gone. It is very well known that almost all the married women have a lover; but it is usual to keep up the forms, as in other nations. I did not, therefore, know what the devil to say. I could not out with the truth, out of regard to her, and I did not choose to lie for my sake;—besides, the thing told itself. I thought the best way would be to let her explain it as she chose (a woman being never at a loss—the devil always sticks by them)—only determining to protect and carry her off, in case of any ferocity on the part of the Signor. I saw that he was quite calm. She went to bed, and next day—how they settled it, I know not, but settle it they did. Well—then I had to explain to Marianna about this never to be sufficiently confounded sister-in-law; which I did by swearing innocence, eternal constancy, &c. &c. …

But the sister-in-law, very much discomposed with being treated in such wise, has (not having her own shame before her eyes) told the affair to half Venice, and the servants (who were summoned by the fight and the fainting) to the other half. But, here, nobody minds such trifles, except to be amused by them. I don't know whether you will be so, but I have scrawled a long letter out of these follies.

Believe me ever. &c.

Originally Letters and Journals of Lord Byron, *George Gordon, Lord Byron, edited by Thomas Moore, John Murray: London, 1830; reproduced in* So Late into the Night, Byron's Letters and Journals, *Vol. 5, edited by Leslie A. Marchand, John Murray, 1976*

The poem reproduced below is probably Byron's best-known lyric. It was sent in another letter to Thomas Moore, when the Venice Carnival was over and Lent had begun, an exhausted renunciation of excess at the end of a long party season. It was apparently inspired by The Jolly Beggar, *an 18th-century Scottish ballad which includes the refrain 'And we'll go no more a roving / Sae late into the night, / And we'll gang nae mair a roving, boys, / Let the moon shine ne'er sae bright'.*

We'll go no more a-roving (1817)
Lord Byron

So, we'll go no more a-roving
So late into the night,
Though the heart be still as loving,
And the moon be still as bright.
For the sword outwears its sheath,
And the soul wears out the breast,
And the heart must pause to breathe,
And love itself have rest.
Though the night was made for loving,
And the day returns too soon,
Yet we'll go no more a-roving
By the light of the moon.

Originally Letters and Journals of Lord Byron, *George Gordon, Lord Byron, edited by Thomas Moore, John Murray: London, 1830.*

CASANOVA

Giacomo Casanova (1725–98) is probably the world's most famous Venetian. And what he is famous for is sex: within a few decades of his death his name had become synonymous with dashing, insatiable, intrigue-laden seduction. The explanation of this fame is more interesting, it lies not so much in the fact that he did it, but in how much he wrote about it: twelve thick volumes of the Histoire de ma Vie *(History of My Life; he wrote in French because more people spoke it than his native Venetian dialect), a superb, self-deprecating, often exciting account of life and manners in 18th-century Europe—in Venice, France, the Netherlands, England, Spain, Rome, St Petersburg, Warsaw—anywhere where there was a court with tables to gamble at, women to sleep with, and nobles to sponge off.*

The son of a Venetian actress (though not, he claimed in later life, of her husband), he was able from an early age to attract the support of wealthy patrons. He finished law school in Padua at the age of 17, and his early career included stints as a clerical lawyer in Venice and Rome, as an officer in the Venetian army (stationed in Corfu and Constantinople), as a professional gambler (unsuccessful), and as a violinist in the orchestra of Venice's San Samuele theatre. By the age of 30 he was in prison, convicted of atheism by the Venetian inquisitors. In fact he was by no means an atheist, but he did supplement a flexible Catholicism with Freemasonry and dabbling in the occult—he said it attracted women and impressed patrons. Given the curious mixture of license and repression that characterised the last decades of the Venetian Republic, these were probably considered sufficient grounds for incarceration. And if not, there were always his infringements of the noble monopoly on control of gambling and, of course, his irrepressible libertinism: his memoirs describe, in some cases in full 18th-century erotic detail, 104 sex scenes. How many are made up, how many real, and how many others are omitted no one knows.

Casanova was imprisoned in the Doge's Palace 'under the leads': the description of his arrest and introduction to his cell is the second extract given below. The story of his escape—the first person ever to do so from that prison—is breathtaking (third extract):

For 18 years thereafter he roamed Europe as an exile, occasionally a rich one when his remarkably modern plans for setting up state lottery schemes succeeded, more often moving on when broke or expelled or both. He wept for joy when he read the pardon granted by the Venetian inquisitors that permitted him to return.

Towards the end of his life, his friends, money and libido more or less exhausted and having himself served as a spy for the inquisitors (he complains of the wantonness of Venetian women with no apparent sense of irony), he became the household librarian for a Bohemian duke. This was fortunate for posterity: his boredom was to spur the writing of his memoirs ('I'm writing my life in order to laugh at myself and I am managing very well.'). It was probably also fortunate that he was far from his beloved Venice: in 1797, the year before his death, it fell to Napoleon, who lost no time in extinguishing the once proud 1,000-year-old Venetian Republic for ever.

History of My Life (1789)
Giacomo Casanova

An adventure

Bad weather having compelled the authorities to postpone the wonderful wedding until the following Sunday, I accompanied M. de Bragadin, who was going to Padua. The amiable old man ran away from the noisy pleasures which no longer suited his age, and he was going to spend in peace the few days which the public rejoicings would have rendered unpleasant for him in Venice. On the following Saturday, after dinner, I bade him farewell, and got into the post-chaise to return to Venice. If I had left Padua two minutes sooner or later, the whole course of my life would have been altered, and my destiny, if destiny is truly shaped by fatal combinations, would have been very different. But the reader can judge for himself.

Having, therefore, left Padua at the very instant marked by fatality, I met at Oriago a cabriolet, drawn at full speed by two post-horses, containing a very pretty woman and a man wearing a German uniform. Within a few yards from me the vehicle was suddenly upset on the side of the river, and the woman, falling over the officer, was in great danger of rolling into the Brenta. I jumped out of my chaise without even stopping my postillion, and rushing to the assistance of the lady I remedied with a chaste hand the disorder caused to her toilet by her fall.

Her companion, who had picked himself up without any injury, hastened towards us, and there was the lovely creature sitting on the ground thoroughly amazed, and less confused from her fall than from the indiscretion of her petticoats, which had exposed in all their nakedness certain parts which an honest woman never shews to a stranger. In the warmth of her thanks, which lasted until her postillion and mine had righted the cabriolet, she often called me her saviour, her guardian angel.

The vehicle being all right, the lady continued her journey towards Padua, and I resumed mine towards Venice, which I reached just in time to dress for the opera.

The next day I masked myself early to accompany the Bucentoro, which, favoured by fine weather, was to be taken to the Lido for the great and ridiculous ceremony. The whole affair is under the responsibility of the admiral of the arsenal, who answers for the weather remaining fine, under penalty of his head, for the slightest contrary wind might capsize the ship and drown the Doge, with all the most serene noblemen, the ambassadors, and the Pope's nuncio, who is the sponsor of that burlesque wedding which the Venetians respect even to superstition. To crown the misfortune of such an accident it would make the whole of Europe laugh, and people would not fail to say that the Doge of Venice had gone at last to consummate his marriage.

I had removed my mask, and was drinking some coffee under the 'procuraties' of St. Mark's Square, when a fine-looking female mask struck me gallantly on the shoulder with her fan. As I did not know who she was I did not take much notice of it, and after I had finished my coffee I put on my mask and walked towards the Spiaggia del Sepulcro, where M. de Bragadin's gondola was waiting for me. As I was getting near the Ponte della Paglia I saw the same masked woman attentively looking at some wonderful monster shewn for a few pence. I went up to her; and asked her why she had struck me with her fan.

'To punish you for not knowing me again after having saved my life.' I guessed that she was the person I had rescued the day before on the banks of the Brenta, and after paying her some compliments I enquired whether she intended to follow the Bucentoro.

'I should like it,' she said, 'if I had a safe gondola.'

I offered her mine, which was one of the largest, and, after consulting a masked person who accompanied her, she accepted. Before stepping in I invited them to take off their masks, but they told me that they wished to remain unknown. I then begged them to tell me if they belonged to the suite of some ambassador, because in that case I should be compelled, much to my regret, to withdraw my invitation; but they assured me that they were both Venetians. The gondola belonging to a patrician, I might have committed myself with the State Inquisitors—a thing which I wished particularly to avoid. We were following the Bucentoro, and seated near the lady I allowed myself a few slight liberties, but she foiled my intentions by changing her seat.

The arrest

While Messer-Grande was thus rummaging among my manuscripts, books and letters, I was dressing myself in an absent-minded manner, neither hurrying myself nor the reverse. I made my toilette, shaved myself, and combed my hair; putting on mechanically a laced shirt and my holiday suit without saying a word, and without Messer-Grande—who did not let me escape his sight for an instant—complaining that I was dressing myself as if I were going to a wedding.

As I went out I was surprised to see a band of forty men-at-arms in the ante-room. They had done me the honour of thinking all these men necessary for my arrest, though, according to the axiom '*Ne Hercules quidem contra duos*', two would have been enough. It is curious that in London, where everyone is brave, only one man is needed to arrest another, whereas in my dear native land, where cowardice prevails, thirty are required. The reason is, perhaps, that the coward on the offensive is more afraid than the coward on the defensive, and thus a man usually cowardly is transformed for the moment into a man of courage. It is certain that at Venice one often sees a man defending himself against twenty *sbirri*, and finally escaping after beating them soundly. I remember once helping a friend of mine at Paris to escape from the hands of forty bum-bailiffs, and we put the whole vile rout of them to flight.

Messer-Grande made me get into a gondola, and sat down near me with an escort of four men. When we came to our destination he offered me coffee, which I refused…

…In course of time the captain of the men-at-arms came to tell me that he was under orders to take me under the Leads. Without a word I followed him. We went by gondola, and after a thousand turnings among the small canals we got into the Grand Canal, and landed at the prison quay. After climbing several flights of stairs we crossed a closed bridge [now the 'Bridge of Sighs'] which forms the communication between the prisons and the Doge's palace, crossing the canal called Rio di Palazzo. On the other side of this bridge there is a gallery which we traversed. We then crossed one room, and entered another, where sat an individual in the dress of a noble, who, after looking fixedly at me, said, '*E quello, mettetelo in deposito*' [This is he, lock him up].

This man was the secretary of the Inquisitors, the prudent Dominic Cavalli, who was apparently ashamed to speak Venetian in my presence as he pronounced my doom in the Tuscan language.

Messer-Grande then made me over to the warden of the Leads, who stood by with an enormous bunch of keys, and accompanied by two guards, made me climb two short flights of stairs, at the top of which followed a passage and then another gallery, at the end of which he opened a door, and I found myself in a dirty garret, thirty-six feet long by twelve broad, badly lighted by a window high up in the roof. I thought this garret was my prison, but I was mistaken; for, taking an enormous key, the gaoler opened a thick door lined with iron, three and a half feet high, with a round hole in the middle, eight inches in diameter, just as I was looking intently at an iron machine. This machine was like a horse shoe, an inch thick and about five inches across from one end to the other. I was thinking what could be the use to which this horrible instrument was put, when the gaoler said, with a smile, 'I see, sir, that you wish to know what that is for, and as it happens I can satisfy your curiosity. When their excellencies give orders that anyone is to be strangled, he is made to sit down on a stool, the back turned to this collar, and his head is so placed that the collar goes round one half of the neck. A silk band, which goes round the other half, passes through this hole, and the two ends are connected with the axle of a wheel which is turned by someone until the prisoner gives up the ghost, for the confessor, God be thanked! never leaves him till he is dead.'

'All this sounds very ingenious, and I should think that it is you who have the honour of turning the wheel.'

He made no answer, and signing to me to enter, which I did by bending double, he shut me up, and afterwards asked me through the grated hole what I would like to eat.

'I haven't thought anything about it yet,' I answered. And he went away, locking all the doors carefully behind him.

The escape

… After having surmounted with the greatest difficulty fifteen or sixteen plates we got to the top, on which I sat astride, Father Balbi [his companion and fellow escapee] imitating my example. Our backs were towards the little island of St. George the Greater [San Giorgio Maggiore], and about two hundred paces in front of us were the numerous cupolas of St. Mark's Church, which forms part of the ducal palace, for St. Mark's is really the Doge's private chapel, and no monarch in the world can boast of having a finer.

My first step was to take off my bundle, and I told my companion to do the same…

After looking about me for some time I told the monk to stay still till I came back, and I set out, my pike in my hand, sitting astride the roof and moving along without any difficulty. For nearly an hour I went to this side and that, keeping a sharp look-out, but in vain; for I could see nothing to which the rope could be fastened, and I was in the greatest perplexity as to what was to be done. It was of no use thinking of getting down on the canal side or by the court of the palace, and the church offered only precipices which led to nothing. To get to the other side of the church towards the Canonica, I should have had to climb roofs so steep that I saw no prospect of success. The situation called for hardihood, but not the smallest piece of rashness…

The Memoirs of Jacques Casanova de Seingalt, *Giacomo Casanova, translated by Arthur Machen, London, 1894. A more recent and fuller translation is* History of My Life, *Giacomo Casanova, translated by Willard R. Trask, Harcourt Inc., 1967.*

WILKIE COLLINS

During his lifetime the novelist and playwright Wilkie Collins (1824–89) was considered the equal of Thackeray and Dickens; afterwards his works quickly faded from public view with his plays never performed and only his most successful novel, The Woman in White *(1860), generally known. However, recently there has been a revival of interest in his work. It is for mysteries and tales involving the supernatural that he is best known. His* The Moonstone *was an early, and much imitated, classic of the new detective novel genre.*

Although 10 years younger than Dickens the two became good friends, Dickens maybe appreciating, even envying, the unconventionality of Collins's life: Collins prided himself on flouting Victorian dress rules and prudery, and although in public he appeared as a bachelor, he kept two separate households. One ménage was with a widow who had kept a neighbouring shop in London, the other was with a Norfolk shepherd's daughter, with whom he had three children. Collins and Dickens visited Italy together in the 1850s, though by the time he wrote The Haunted Hotel: a Mystery of Modern Venice *(1879) Collins was no longer writing for the Dickens periodicals (which also serialised Dickens's own work). A melodrama combining aristocrats, the supernatural, and ghoulish deeds' just deserts, it found a ready readership in the late Victorian world.*

In the extracts below, the scene is set for the deceased duke's decaying, severed head to start floating around the cursed Room Fourteen, giving off a decidedly nasty smell.

The Haunted Hotel: A Mystery of Modern Venice (1879)
Wilkie Collins

The Palace Hotel, appealing for encouragement mainly to English
and American travellers, celebrated the opening of its doors, as a
matter of course, by the giving of a grand banquet, and the deliv-
ery of a long succession of speeches.

Delayed on his journey, Henry Westwick only reached Venice
in time to join the guests over their coffee and cigars. Observing
the splendour of the reception rooms, and taking note especially
of the artful mixture of comfort and luxury in the bedchambers,
he began to share the old nurse's view of the future, and to contemplate seriously the coming dividend of ten per cent. The hotel
was beginning well, at all events. So much interest in the enterprise had been aroused, at home and abroad, by profuse adver-
tising, that the whole accommodation of the building had been
secured by travellers of all nations for the opening night. Henry
only obtained one of the small rooms on the upper floor, by a
lucky accident—the absence of the gentleman who had written to
engage it. He was quite satisfied, and was on his way to bed, when
another accident altered his prospects for the night, and moved
him into another and a better room.

Ascending on his way to the higher regions as far as the first
floor of the hotel, Henry's attention was attracted by an angry
voice protesting, in a strong New England accent, against one of
the greatest hardships that can be inflicted on a citizen of the
United States—the hardship of sending him to bed without gas
in his room.

The Americans are not only the most hospitable people to be
found on the face of the earth—they are (under certain conditions) the most patient and good-tempered people as well. But
they are human; and the limit of American endurance is found
in the obsolete institution of a bedroom candle. The American
traveller, in the present case, declined to believe that his bedroom
was in a complete finished state without a gas-burner. The man-

ager pointed to the fine antique decorations (renewed and regilt) on the walls and the ceiling, and explained that the emanations of burning gas-light would certainly spoil them in the course of a few months. To this the traveller replied that it was possible, but that he did not understand decorations. A bedroom with gas in it was what he was used to, was what he wanted, and was what he was determined to have. The compliant manager volunteered to ask some other gentleman, housed on the inferior upper storey (which was lit throughout with gas), to change rooms. Hearing this, and being quite willing to exchange a small bedchamber for a large one, Henry volunteered to be the other gentleman. The excellent American shook hands with him on the spot. 'You are a cultured person, sir,' he said; 'and you will no doubt understand the decorations.'

Henry looked at the number of the room on the door as he opened it. The number was Fourteen.

Tired and sleepy, he naturally anticipated a good night's rest. In the thoroughly healthy state of his nervous system, he slept as well in a bed abroad as in a bed at home. Without the slightest assignable reason, however, his just expectations were disappointed. The luxurious bed, the well-ventilated room, the delicious tranquillity of Venice by night, all were in favour of his sleeping well. He never slept at all. An indescribable sense of depression and discomfort kept him waking through darkness and daylight alike. He went down to the coffee-room as soon as the hotel was astir, and ordered some breakfast. Another unaccountable change in himself appeared with the appearance of the meal. He was absolutely without appetite. An excellent omelette, and cutlets cooked to perfection, he sent away untasted—he, whose appetite never failed him, whose digestion was still equal to any demands on it!

The day was bright and fine. He sent for a gondola, and was rowed to the Lido. Out on the airy Lagoon, he felt like a new man. He had not left the hotel ten minutes before he was fast asleep in the gondola. Waking, on reaching the landing-place, he crossed the Lido, and enjoyed a morning's swim in the Adriatic. There was only a poor restaurant on the island, in those days; but his appetite was now ready for anything; he ate whatever was offered to him, like a famished man. He could hardly believe, when he reflected on it, that he had sent away untasted his excellent breakfast at the hotel.

Returning to Venice, he spent the rest of the day in the picture-galleries and the churches. Towards six o'clock his gondola took him back, with another fine appetite, to meet some travelling acquaintances with whom he had engaged to dine at the table d'hôte.

The dinner was deservedly rewarded with the highest approval by every guest in the hotel but one. To Henry's astonishment, the appetite with which he had entered the house mysteriously and completely left him when he sat down to table. He could drink some wine, but he could literally eat nothing. 'What in the world is the matter with you?' his travelling acquaintances asked. He could honestly answer, 'I know no more than you do.'

When night came, he gave his comfortable and beautiful bedroom another trial. The result of the second experiment was a repetition of the result of the first. Again he felt the all-pervading sense of depression and discomfort. Again he passed a sleepless night. And once more, when he tried to eat his breakfast, his appetite completely failed him!

This personal experience of the new hotel was too extraordinary to be passed over in silence. Henry mentioned it to his friends in the public room, in the hearing of the manager. The manager, naturally zealous in defence of the hotel, was a little hurt at the implied reflection cast on Number Fourteen. He invited the travellers present to judge for themselves whether Mr. Westwick's bedroom was to blame for Mr. Westwick's sleepless nights; and he especially appealed to a grey-headed gentleman, a guest at the breakfast-table of an English traveller, to take the lead in the investigation. 'This is Doctor Bruno, our first physician in Venice,' he explained. 'I appeal to him to say if there are any unhealthy influences in Mr. Westwick's room.' Introduced to Number Fourteen, the doctor looked round him with a certain appearance of interest which was noticed by everyone present. 'The last time I was in this room,' he said, 'was on a melancholy occasion. It was before the palace was changed into an hotel. I was in professional attendance on an English nobleman who died here.' One of the persons present inquired the name of the nobleman. Doctor Bruno answered (without the slightest suspicion that he was speaking before a brother of the dead man), 'Lord Montbarry.' Henry quietly left the room, without saying a word to anybody. He was not, in any sense of the term, a superstitious man. But he felt, nevertheless, an insurmountable reluctance to remaining in the hotel. He decided on leaving Venice.

Originally The Haunted Hotel: A Mystery of Modern Venice, *Wilkie Collins, Chatto & Windus, 1879; now available from Nonsuch Publishing, 2007.*

GASPARO CONTARINI

Gasparo Contarini (1483–1542) was born into a patrician Venetian family and he studied at what was then Venice's own university, that of Padua, between 1501 and 1509. He was a follower of Aristotle and, at this time in his life, believed that human reason, rather than simply acquiescence in faith, was the best way of arriving at truth. Then came Venice's massive and unexpected defeat by the French in 1509 at Agnadello, during the wars of the Holy League established by Pope Julius II to curb Venetian power. The defeat seems to have brought on a personal crisis for Contarini. He was overwhelmed by a sense of helplessness and became more convinced that only through a life of pure virtue and Christian observance could one confront the reality of a hostile world. He was also troubled by the rise of Protestantism but felt that it was the arrogance of papal power which had been one of its causes. He thus occupied an ambiguous position in the Church. While a later pope, Paul III, was sympathetic enough to make him a cardinal (1535) and accept his critical text on Church corruption, the next pope, Paul IV, placed the same work on the index of banned books.

Contarini was tempted towards spiritual withdrawal and a life of philosophical contemplation but a stronger impulse was his belief in serving his city. He was Venetian ambassador to the court of the Habsburg emperor Charles V and a governor of the city of Brescia, one of Venice's mainland possessions. When in favour with the pope he engaged in diplomatic activity for the Church. His intellect, balanced views and personal integrity made him highly respected. His last years were clouded by the increasing conservatism of the Church and by the condemnation of many of his friends by the papal Inquisition.

Contarini's Commonwealth and Government of Venice was written in tumultuous times, in 1520, but only published after his death in 1543. He was writing for a subdued audience that had seen the greatness of Venice diminished by her humiliations on the mainland. Contarini focused, however, on her enduring qualities. Just as the Romans had defeated the Greeks militarily but the Greeks had remained the superior civilisation, so too Venice would remain culturally superior to her enemies. He used Aristotelian models of good government to suggest that Venice's consitution was perfectly balanced between a mon-

arch (the doge), a nobility and her citizens. She had reached a maturity which made her supreme over less favoured rivals.

The following extract comes from the first English translation of the book (1599) and shows how the doge exercised hospitality and ceremony to cement the allegiance of Venice's citizens to the state.

The Commonwealth and Government of Venice (1520)
Gasparo Contarini

The Prince therefore being honored with this kingly apparance and shewe, because oftentimes it fell out that private wealth suffised not to maintayne so great dignity and pompe: there is allowed unto the Duke out of the common treasure yearely, three thousand and five hundred crownes of gold: ...Hee alwaies useth costly garments: he dwelleth in a pallace wonderfully adorned with goodly chambers and tapistry, abounding with vessels of silver and all other such furniture, as is beseeming the degree of a prince. Foure times a yeare he maketh a solemne and sumptuous banket, to above threescore citizens, the same being ordered and set forth with all the magnificency that may be. Wherin our predecessors brought into our commonwealth the auncient order of the inhabitantes of Lacedemon and Crete (whose commonwealthes were noble and glorious) but with a much better moderation and order: for they because they thought the often meeting of the citizens was a mean to combine them together in friendship, instituted certaine publike feastes at the charge of the common treasure, to which the citizens assembling had meanes one to be acquainted with the other, and withal by so friendly a meeting to confirm a new friendship. Foure times a yeare therfore are the citizens banqueted of the prince, with fare truely honorable and daintie, and yet for the exceedingness thereof not to be envied: neyther doth every one come unorderly as it pleaseth him, but those whome the prince shall vouchsafe to call: unlesse it bee the Counsellors, the Advocators, the Presidents of the xl. men, & the Presidents of the tennes, who in preheminence of their offices, are usually present at the princes bankets: the other citizens come not but invited.

These foure feastings are in this sort divided, that the elder and worthiest citizens being invited, doe in the winter time upon S. Stephen's day assemble themselves in the publike pallace appointed for the princes habitation, and with a solemne pompe waite upon the prince from thence to the church of S. Marke, and there bee present with him at Masse, which being ended, then they waite upon him backe to his house againe, and there be pertakers of his banquet. Likewise in the moneth of Aprill on the day of Saint Marke (whose memory is with exceeding honour solemnized of the Venetians, as entituling him their patron and defender, ever since thc reliques of his body were brought unto Venice, from north of Alexandria a noble Citie of Aegypt) the cittizens of lesse age and dignitie invited of the prince, doe in like manner (after the solemnities in the church are ended) convay him home and dine with him.

Thirdly, uppon Ascension day, being the day of the great fayer at Venice, they are invited and admitted to the Princes banket, that are fully arrived and entred into that age which we call Virilis or mans estate. These also doe early in the morning waite upon the Duke from his house, and go aborde a ship gorgeously trimmed and set forth, reserved onely to that use, and is by the Venetians called Bucentoro: so soone as they are passed the marshes and come to behold the plaine and open sea, by an ancient indulgence of the high Bishops ...the prince throwing a ring of golde into the sea, useth in a manncr these speaches, that with that ring hee doeth betroth himselfe to the sea, in token of a true and perpetuall Empyre. To this there are added certayne ceremonies by the Patriarch of the Cittie, which being ended, they lande at the Church dedicated to Saynt Nicholaus, a thing of great antiquitie, built uppon that shore or banke which divideth the sea from the lakes. There the holy misteries are celebrated, which being ended, they go aborde the ship againe, and returne to Venice, attending on the Prince home to his house, where they dyne with him.

The fourth and last banquette pertayneth to the young citti-zens, who the twelve Kalendes of Iuly, on the day dedicated to the two Martyres Vitus and Modestus, doe with solemne pompe wayte upon the Prince to the Temple of those Martirs, which is situate neere to the great channell that divideth the cittie in the middest: which channel is for that tyme conjoyned with a bridge made upon two galleyes, least otherwise to make that journey, would cost a very long and laboursome circuit and compasse. The church being visited, and the solemnities in the church fin-ished, they attend upon the prince home to his pallace, where they are received with a royall and magnificent banket. There are to these bankets admitted dauncers, jesters, and excellent singers, to recreate & delight the guestes, and withal certaine sports and playes are intermingled, which doe move exceeding mirth and pleasure: and this ancient custome is still observed in the com-monwealth of Venice, though somewhat moderated. For by this means the citizens in a manner of every degree, yea equals with equalles are entertayned at the princes table: which seemeth ex-ceedingly well ordered and disposed as well for the dignity of the prince, as also for nourishing & maintayning love and good will among the citizens. But because every citizen that is a gentleman, cannot every yeare receive this grace of being invited, it is by an olde law ordained, least any one should seeme to be left out, that the prince should in the winter time sende to every citizen that hath priviledge of voyce in the greater Councell five wild duckes, as a portion or share of the publike banket, which likewise is a great meane to the Duke of winning the love and goodwill of the citizens. In these chargeable expences doth the Duke yearely con-sume and spend a great part of that money which hee receiveth out of the common treasure: so that though the Duke would be covetous, yet cannot hee in a manner staine with any basenesse the noblenesse & dignity of the place he holdeth.

The Commonwealth and Government of Venice, *Gasparo Contarini, 1520, translated by Lewis Lewkenor, 1599.*

BARON CORVO
(FREDERICK ROLFE)

An accomplished and eccentric writer, but a deeply flawed character, Frederick Rolfe (1860–1913) was one of the oddest—and most importunate—foreigners ever to have settled in Venice. 'Settled' is hardly the correct word since he alternated between living in pensiones, lodging with hospitable friends (who invariably came to regret their hospitality), dossing for weeks on end in a boat on the lagoon tormented (he claimed) by fleets of swimming rats, and on occasions wandering the beaches of the Lido, homeless, in winter.

Rolfe, who liked early in his life to style himself 'Baron Corvo'—a title he claimed had been bestowed on him in Rome by the widowed Duchess Sforza-Cesarini—first came to Venice in the summer of 1907, when he was 47 years old, and lived most of the remaining six years of his life in the city. For much of that time he had no money and lived by relentlessly importuning support from other English residents, whose only thanks for their help was to find themselves pilloried in his bizarre romance, The Desire and Pursuit of the Whole, from which the following extracts are taken.

The book's title is a reference to Plato's concept, advanced in the Symposium, of the union of complementary opposites in love. It is a love story, containing much autobiographical material. Rolfe was pedantically self-centred; he was also homosexual, with a confessed weakness for Venetian gondoliers. The romance, written in a hectic, often self-consciously telegrammatic prose, full of colour and allusion, describes Rolfe's life in Venice, and his love for the city and lagoon, through the person of Nicholas Crabbe (read 'Rolfe') who comes to Venice with a young girl whom he has saved from the 1908 earthquake in Messina, and who becomes his faithful servant, his gondolier, and finally his lover. But nothing is straightforward with Rolfe: the girl—referred to mostly as a 'boy'—is to all intents and purposes a 'strapping male', although technically a girl. Fantasy was a vital element in both Rolfe's life and his writing. In his best-known fictional work, Hadrian the Seventh, the hero, George Arthur Rose (again, read 'Rolfe'), becomes elected pope in Rome, and begins on an ambitious project of setting the Catholic world to rights. In real life, Rolfe, who liked to sign

*himself 'Fr. Rolfe' as though he were ordained, had been ejected early
on from his seminary in Rome for 'lack of vocation'.*

*Although perhaps preposterous as a personality, these extracts show
Rolfe to be an engaging writer nonetheless, with a considerable knowledge of the Venetian boat culture with which he so curiously identified.
The first describes the Venetian childhood of the young girl, Ermenegilda, also called Zilda, whom the protagonist, Nicholas Crabbe, has
saved from the earthquake. In the second extract Crabbe takes her
to a hotel as his servant, though she is now Zildo and definitely male.*

The Desire and Pursuit of the Whole
(1909, published posthumously in 1934)
Frederick Rolfe, Baron Corvo

Her father had been a gondoliere and gastaldo of the Traghetto of the
Trinity in Venice, as also his parents had been before him. …Nicho-
las was slightly puzzled about this strange 'Traghetto della Trinità.'
He had thought that he knew all the Venetian ferries. And it was not
till after his return to Venice that he discovered it to be the antique
name (only used now by gondolieri) of the well-known Traghetto
della Salute. How antique? Well, as antique as this. In 1256, the
Serene Republic gave the then antique church and monastery of The
Trinity to the Order of Teutonic Knights in payment for their services
against Genova. After three hundred and thirty-six years, Pope Clem-
ent the Eighth suppressed that Trinity Priory of Teutonic Knights in
1592, and moved to it the patriarchal Seminary from San Cipriano
di Murano. And, thirty-nine years later, the patriarchal seminary was
shunted a little farther up the island to its present site, so that the
Serene Republic might erect the great church of Santa Maria della
Salute on the old Trinity Priory in thanksgiving for deliverance from
the plague of 1631. Naturally a name, which has been embedded in
human memory more than three hundred and seventy-five years,
still persists after the lapse of a mere two hundred and sixty.

Ermenegilda continued, describing her first nine years of this life in the parish of Sanstefano, alone, with Bastian her father in his little house of four rooms (full of nut-wood bedsteads and antique pictures as large as walls) in the tiny court called Malatin which lies just under the distorted bell-tower of Sanstefano. Outside that parish, all the rest of the terra firma of Venice, excepting the Square of Saint Mark and his basilica and the markets of Rialto, seemed quite unknown by her: but her acquaintance with the city's labyrinth of waterways was of the most intimate nature.

The first thing which she had in memory occurred on a certain Lord's Day when she was about three years old. She and Bastian her father were eating cherries on the doorstep; and he picked her up, laughing, and jetted her into the canal, saying, like this, that he would give her a coral for her neck if she swam the length of the gondola which by chance was moored thereby. At which she took fear: but she contrived to swim the course; and she won the coral—the same coral which this cruel earthquake ravished from her. And she flushed, flashing a quick glance at Nicholas.

There was nothing much more to tell. No: she never played with other children. Bastian forbade it, saying, like this, that no one was fit to speak to his Zildo. He always called her 'Zildo' or '*fio mio*' [my son]: because he preferred making her a son rather than a daughter. That was why she never wore any but boys' clothes during her father's life-time; and, in Venice, she always passed for a boy. … [Her father] taught her to read in the prayer-book, and to write her name, and to cook and sew like a gondoliere. Naturally the polishing of the gondola became her job, as soon as she could row. When? She could not clearly remember: but it must have been soon after the time when she found that she was able to swim…

And, when she became larger and more expert, of course she always rowed the poop-oar while Bastian rowed at the prow, when rich forestiers [foreigners] wished to have two oars to take them to the glass makers of Murano or the lace-makers of Burano, or Torxelo, or Saint Francis-in-the-Wilds, or Saint George-in-the-Seaweed, or Saint Angel-in-Dust, or the Lido, or other islets. In this way they earned many deniers, never less than three franchi a day and sometimes as many as thirty when they put the gilded apparatus into the poppe for some rich lordo who desiderated a gondola of luxury.

The Albergo Bellavista in Venice is so called because (from the front windows) you do get a most beautiful view of the Square of Saint Mark to your right, and the façade of Saint Mark's to your left, and (in front of you) the Campanile and the Piazzetta with its Columns and the Basin of Saint Mark with the distant islands of Sanzorzi [San Giorgio] and Spinalonga [the Giudecca]. …The first thing which flapped his return in his face was the hellish excess of temperature. Modern comfort (as advertised) means (to Venetian Boniface) arid stifling heat of 80° Fahr. from hot-water pipes and windows hermetically sealed. The hotel was all but empty. But he could not have his old rooms, as that floor was occupied by a gentleman who was well known in Venice, his lady, her baby, its bonne. People were always upsetting Crabbe somehow. The rooms which he wanted were at the top, one on each side of a corridor-end; and there were two windows in each, which gave on a terrace commanding the eponymous fine view. He was annoyed, because these seemed to be the only rooms where he could regulate his own temperature by the windows, without being walked on by Germans. It oozed out, though, that there was another room on the same level, with nearly the same outlook: but, disgraceful to say, it was in an unheated part of the house unused during winter. 'For the Love of God transport me thither instantly,' gasped Crabbe, sweating, headaching, and the odour of hot-iron pipes scratching his nostrils. It was a smaller room, No. 26, on the top floor approached by a side-stair, having two big windows, and a terrace adjoining his former one. Two tiny bedrooms were on the same landing, one of which would suit his servant; and he made a bargain for L.16 a day all complete. This for the present. After a week, he would reconsider his plans. The plump little proprietor feared that he would be cold. 'Nonsense,' Crabbe snapped, 'we shall be out all day, and only use the rooms for sleeping; and we shall sleep with wide windows: So just give us four blankets apiece, and a couple of hot-water bottles in each bed every evening at 20 o'clock punctually and I don't want to hear any more about pulmonitis,' he concluded…

Crabbe remembered that he had left his servant upstairs, uninstructed. He ran up. The boy was poised by the landing-window, observing a pair of facchini who made the two rooms ready for habitation. No words had been exchanged: Zildo's air sternly prohibited even the passing of the time of day, and the facchini laboured in full consciousness of being but worms of dust. Crabbe told the boy to unpack his luggage when the rooms were ready and then to come to him in the hall.

…Zildo came down; and Nicholas rushed him through Merceria to Barbaro's by Rialto for an outfit, a bag of his own, a couple of blue serge reefer jackets and trousers of a better cut and quality than those scratched up at Gerace, half a dozen white woollen high-collared guernseys, and a sufficiency of underclothes, handkerchiefs and boots with a plain toilet box. To these he added a couple of shiny-peaked caps from Semini's; and made the boy look (as he himself did) like an unpretending junior officer of the mercantile marine in mufti…

Directly after luncheon, the two went to the squero of Grassi by Sanzanipolo [SS. Giovanni e Paolo] to get the pupparin. A pupparin is a smaller bark than a gondola, six to eight metres long against the other's eleven and without the twisted-up steel-armed fore and aft. It is flat-bottomed, like a gondola; and has the same curious but calculated curve in length, the same excess on the right which balances the weight of the gondoliere poised high on the left. Its prow is sharply beaked: its poop (from which it takes its name) is pertly spread and tilted like the tail of a merle at moments. Crabbe's pupparin was very long and slim: it would carry one passenger in ease with three oarsmen at pleasure. He always took three oars and three forcole [rowlocks]: for (as he said) you never know what may happen—and squalls had been known to tear his craft from moorings to an oar stuck in the mud; and, but for the extra ones, he might have drifted idiotically.

He was pleased with the look of this slim ship. It was black and smart and polished, and promised speed. Grassi had pitched and tallowed it without, and painted it within; and had fitted it with new gleaming-white floor-boards, and new oars and forcole nicely oiled and brown. It had none of the rumpled carpets or greasy brass-work or dusty cushions or funeral palls beloved of Venetians…the bark was bare, built for use and stripped for speed. Zildo surveyed it, as the squeraiuoli launched it on rollers into the stinking canal: the Rio dei Mendicanti, where the Ospedal Xivile is, has quite the most fancy stench in Venice at all seasons of the year and at all stages of the tide. Zildo eyed the pupparin as one who knows what should be, and is satisfied. The winter afternoon was bright and sunny as most Venetian winter afternoons are.

'Row at the poop; and let us go on the lagoon beyond Sanzorzi,' said Nicholas, as he took the prow-oar.

It was not far, after exciting twists through small canals into Rio della Canonica, under the Bridge of Sighs, and out to the Basin of Saint Mark. No collisions actually occurred. At the angle, where the angel closes the hole in the wall by which the ape-devil bolted there was a narrow squeak of one: but Nicholas remembered that seven years had lapsed since Zildo wriggled a bark through the city intricacies, and felt that the present test was severe.

…'Sior,' said Zildo, 'it is very different rowing in these narrow crowded ditches after the open sea of Calabria: but I shall do better tomorrow, and still better next week.'

'It goes very well,' answered Nicholas: 'and now, uoa! uoa! regata!'

Both bounded at the oars; and the pupparin hissed like a javelin across the broad basin, where steam-ferries pass from Canalazzo to the Lido, and Austrian excursion boats anchor in seven or eight metres of water. Between the islands of Sanzorzi and Spinalonga Nicholas knew that he rowed before the forcefullest and featliest gondoliere who ever had rowed behind him.

The Desire and Pursuit of the Whole, *Frederick Rolfe, Baron Corvo,* *Cassell & Co., 1953.*

THOMAS CORYATE

Thomas Coryate (1577–1617; also spelled Coryat and Coriat, and known to all his friends as Tom) was a great enthusiast, eccentric, wit and intrepid traveller. He wrote and entertained all the way from his home in the village of Odcombe, Somerset, where his father was the vicar, via Winchester and Oxford, where he studied; via London, where he joined the Prince of Wales's household; and finally to Gujarat in India, where he died of dysentery in 1617. He walked most of the way between England and India, often at a prodigious pace, covering the ground between Jerusalem and Delhi (about 3,300 miles) in ten months on a budget of a penny a day, travelling with various pilgrim and other caravans. His habit of denouncing Islam to fellow travellers occasionally got him into trouble, as did his preaching Christianity to a rabbi in the ghetto in Venice some years earlier; on that occasion the British ambassador Sir Henry Wotton (q.v.), had to send his gondola to rescue him.

In Coryate's day English was scarcely spoken outside the British Isles. Like scholars for the previous 1,000 years, Coryate was able to use Latin for most of his European travels, but as he proceeded East he also learned Italian and Turkish, and later Arabic and Persian. He showed his skill, or at least his charm, in this last by earning 100 silver rupees from the Persian Emperor Jahangir for an oration in his honour.

But before his great final journey—he left England in 1612 for Constantinople and thence to India—he toured Europe for six months in 1608, also much of it on foot. This proto-Grand Tour included six weeks in Venice and was written up in his book, Coryate's Crudities (1611), whose aim was to encourage continental travel and which was very popular at the time. It is an enormous work, earnestly recording his experiences and offering advice for travellers, fearlessly reaching places the other guide books did not reach: lost and walking alone across Germany's Black Forest he encountered his only threat of violence when a peasant remonstrated with him for eating grapes from his vines. In Venice he boldly recorded his visit to a courtesan's palace (being Coryate he does not end his description with 'I made my excuses and left', but 'I did endeavour by persuasive terms to convert her'—he failed).

Here he is on the subject of the porphyry sculptured groups on the corner of the south façade of St Mark's (they are now known as the 'Tetrarchs' and are thought to be 4th-century Egyptian), on his visit to a Venetian courtesan, and on leaving Venice.

Coryate's Crudities (1611)
Thomas Coryate

On the Tetrarchs

There is a third thing to be seen in that place [St Mark's Square], which is very worthy your observation, being near to the foresaid gallows, and portrayed in the corner of the wall as you go into the Duke's Palace. The portraits of four noble gentlemen of Albania that were brothers, which are made in porphyry stone with their falchions by their sides, and each couple consulting privately together by themselves, of whom this notable history following is reported.

These noble brothers came from Albania together in a ship laden with great store of riches. After their arrival at Venice, which was the place whereunto they were bound, two of them went on shore and left the other two in the ship. The two that were landed entered into a consultation and conspiracy how they might dispatch their other brothers which remained in the ship, to the end they might gain all the riches to themselves. Whereupon, they bought themselves some drugs to that purpose, and determined at a banquet to present the same to their other brothers in a potion or otherwise. Likewise, on the other side, those two brothers that were left in the ship whispered secretly amongst themselves how they might make away their brothers that were landed, that they might get all the wealth to themselves. And thereupon procured means accordingly. At last this was the final issue of these consultations. They that had been at land presented to their other brothers certain poisoned drugs at a banquet to the end to kill them. Which those brothers did eat and died therewith, but not incontinently. For before they died they ministered a certain poisoned marchpane [marzipan] or some such other thing at the very same banquet to their brothers that had been at land. Both which poisons when they had thoroughly wrought their effects upon both couples, all four died shortly after. Whereupon, the Signiory of Venice seized upon all their goods as their own, which was the first treasure that ever Venice possessed, and the first occasion of enriching the estate; and in memorial of that uncharitable and unbrotherly conspiracy have erected the portraits of them in porphyry, as I said before in two several couples consulting together.

On the famous Venetian courtesans

For so infinite are the allurements of these amorous calypsoes, that the fame of them has drawn many to Venice from some of the remotest parts of Christendom, to contemplate their beauties, and enjoy their pleasing dalliances. And indeed such is the variety of the delicious objects they minister to their lovers that they want nothing tending to delight. For when you come into one of their palaces (as indeed some few of the principalest of them live in very magnificent and portly buildings fit for the entertainment of a great prince) you seem to enter into the paradise of Venus. For their fairest rooms are most glorious and glittering to behold. The walls round about being adorned with most sumptuous tapestry and gilt leather. Besides you may see the picture of the noble courtesan most exquisitely drawn. As for herself she comes to you decked like the Queen and goddess of love, in so much that you will think she made a late transmigration from Paphos, Cnidus, or Cythera, the ancient habitations of dame Venus. For her face is adorned with the quintessence of beauty. In her cheeks you shall see the lily and the rose strive for the supremacy, and the silver tramels of her hair displayed in that curious manner besides her two frizzled peaks, standing up like pretty pyramids, that they give you the true cos amoris. But if you have an exact judgement, you may easily discern the effects of those famous apothecary drugs heretofore used amongst the noble ladies of Rome, even stibium, cerusa, and purpurissum. For few of the courtesans are so much beholding to nature, but that they adulterate their faces, and supply her defect with one of these three. A thing so common amongst them that many of them which have an elegant natural beauty do varnish their faces (the observation whereof made me not a little pity their vanities) with these kind of sordid trumperies. Wherein methinks they seem *ebur atramento candefacere*, according to that excellent proverb of Plautus: that is, to make ivory white with ink.

Also the ornaments of her body are so rich, that except you do even geld your affections (a thing hardly to be done) or carry with you Ulysses' herb called moly, which is mentioned by Homer, that is, some antidote against those venereous titillations, she will very near benumb and captivate your senses, and make reason vale bonnet to affection. For you shall see her decked with many chains of gold and orient pearl, like a second Cleopatra (but they are very little), divers gold rings beautified with diamonds and other costly stones, jewels in both her ears of great worth. A gown of damask (I speak this of the nobler courtesans) either decked with a deep gold fringe or laced with five or six gold laces, each two inches broad. Her petticoat of red camlet edged with rich gold fringe, stockings of carnation silk, her breath and her whole body, the more to enamour you, most fragrantly perfumed. Though these things will at the first sight seem unto you most delectable allurements, yet if you shall rightly weigh them in the scales of a mature judgement, you will say with the wise man, and that very truly, that they are like a golden ring in a swine's snout.

Moreover, she will endeavour to enchant you partly with her melodious notes that she warbles out upon her lute, which she fingers with as laudable a stroke as many men that are excellent professors in the noble science of music; and partly with that heart-tempting harmony of her voice. Also you will find the Venetian courtesan (if she be a selected woman indeed) a good rhetorician and a most elegant discourser, so that if she cannot move you with all these foresaid delights, she will assay your constancy with her rhetorical tongue. And to the end she may minister unto you the stronger temptations to come to her lure, she will show you her chamber of recreation, where you shall see all manner of pleasing objects, as many fair painted coffers wherewith it is garnished round about, a curious milk-white canopy of needle work, a silk quilt embroidered with gold: and generally all her bedding sweetly perfumed. And amongst other amiable ornaments she will show you one thing only in her chamber tending to mortification, a matter strange amongst so many *irritamenta malorum*, even the picture of Our Lady by her bedside, with Christ in her arms, placed within a crystal glass. But beware notwithstanding all these *illecebrae et lenocinia amoris*, that you enter not into terms of private conversation with her. For then you shall find her such a one as Lipsius truly calls her, *callidam et calidam solis filiam*, that is, the crafty and hot daughter of the sun.

Moreover, I will tell you this news which is most true, that if you should wantonly converse with her, and not give her that *salarium iniquitatis* [wages of sin], which you had promised her, but perhaps cunningly escape from her company, she will either cause your throat to be cut by her ruffiano if he can after catch you in the city, or procure you to be arrested (if you are to be found) and clapped up in the prison, where you shall remain till you have paid her all you did promise her…

There is one most notable thing more to be mentioned concerning these Venetian courtesans, with the relation whereof I will end this discourse of them. If any of them happen to have children (as indeed they have but few, for according to the old proverb the best carpenters make the fewest chips) they are brought up either at their own charge or in a certain house of the city appointed for no other use but only for the bringing up of the courtesans bastards, which I saw eastward above St Marks street near to the sea side. In the south wall of which building that looks towards the sea, I observed a certain iron gate inserted into a hollow piece of the wall, betwixt which grate and a plain stone beneath it, there is a convenient little space to put in an infant…

Thus have I described unto you the Venetian courtesans, but because I have related so many particulars of them, as few Englishmen that have lived many years in Venice can do the like, or at least if they can they will not upon their return into England, I believe you will cast an aspersion of wantonness upon me, and say that I could not know all these matters without my own experience. I answer you, that although I might have known them without my experience, yet for my better satisfaction, I went to one of their nobler houses (I will confess) to see the manner of their life and observe their behaviour; …rather as *Panaetius* did to *Thais*, of whom we read that when he came to her, and craved a secret room for his pastime, she should answer him that the same room where they were together was secret enough, because nobody could see them but only God. Upon which speech the godly man took occasion to persuade her to the fear of God and religion, and to the reformation of her licentious life, since God was able to pry into the secretest corners of the world. And so at last converted her by this means from a wanton courtesan to a holy and religious woman. In like manner I both wished the conversion of the courtesan that I saw, and did my endeavour by persuasive terms to convert her, though my speeches could not take the like effect that those of *Panaetius* did.

Neither can I be persuaded that it ought to be esteemed for a stain or blemish to the reputation of an honest and ingenuous man to see a courtesan in her house, and note her manners and conversation, because according to the old maxim, *cognitio mali non est mala*, the knowledge of evil is not evil, …so did I visit the palace of a noble courtesan, view her own amorous person, hear her talk, observe her fashion of life, and yet was nothing contaminated therewith, nor corrupted in manner. Therefore, I instantly request you (most candid reader) to be as charitably conceited of me, though I have at large deciphered and as it were anatomised a Venetian courtesan unto you, as you would have me of yourself upon the like request.

On his departure from Venice

And so at length I finish the treatise of this incomparable city, this most beautiful Queen, this untainted virgin, this paradise, this Tempe, this rich diadem and most flourishing garland of Christendom: of which the inhabitants may as proudly vaunt, as I have read the Persians have done of their Ormus, who say that if the world were a ring, then should Ormus be the gem thereof. The same (I say) may the Venetians speak of their city, and much more truly. The sight whereof has yielded unto me such infinite and unspeakable contentment (I must needs confess) that even as Albertus, Marquis of Gualdo, said (as I have before spoken) were he put to his choice to be Lord of four of the fairest cities of Italy, or the arsenal of Venice, he would prefer the arsenal. In the like manner I say, that had there been an offer made unto me before I took my journey to Venice, either that four of the richest manors of Somersetshire (wherein I was born) should be gratis bestowed upon me if I never saw Venice, or neither of them if I should see it; although certainly those manors would do me much more good in respect of a state of livelihood to live in the world, than the sight of Venice: yet notwithstanding I will ever say while I live that the sight of Venice and her resplendent beauty, antiquities, and monuments has by many degrees more contented my mind, and satisfied my desires, then those four lordships could possibly have done.

Thus much of the glorious city of Venice.

Coryate's Venice (taken from Coryate's Crudities; *1611), edited by John Pitt, The Beeches Press, 1989.*

CHARLES DICKENS

During his lifetime Charles Dickens (1812–70) was already one of the most-read novelists in the English language, a position he has retained more or less ever since. A restless workaholic and natural showman, his depictions of poverty and of the injustice of poverty in Victorian Britain gave powerful impetus to the movement for social reform (G.B. Shaw called Little Dorrit *'a more seditious book than* Das Kapital*').*

Etching from the book *Portrait Gallery of Eminent Men and Women in Europe and America,* published in 1873.

Dickens was much affected by his childhood experience of the fall from gentility to penury when his spendthrift civil servant father was imprisoned in the Marshalsea debtors' prison. Dickens was 12, and had found work pasting labels onto pots of blacking—sometimes in a shop window just off London's Strand where a crowd would form to watch the small boys working—and lived alone in squalid lodgings (the rest of the family lived somewhat more comfortably in the prison). On his father's release he went to school, but then at the age of 15 was again obliged to find work, this time as a solicitor's clerk, a position that was less irksome and provided plenty of material for his novels.

Despite his enormous success in his own lifetime—reputational and commercial—he was never able to exorcise his personal demon, urging him to make money to escape the poverty of his childhood. A generous man, this need was exacerbated by an ever-growing circle of relatives financially dependent on him, which later came to include a young actress mistress and her family. When in his fifties he discovered he could combine the superb characterisations in his novels with his love of acting by giving fabulously well-paid public readings, he literally worked himself to death, throwing himself into a punishing schedule of performances in which he read and acted passages from his novels, reducing entire audiences—and himself—alternately to tears and joyous laughter: As one audience member put it, 'He seemed to be physically transformed as he passed from one character to another … he stood before us as a magician. When he sat down it was not mere applause that followed, but a passionate outburst of love for the man.' He visited Venice twice. The result of his first visit in 1845 was a somewhat un-original passage on Venice in his Pictures from Italy *(1846), mostly about the dungeons in the Doge's Palace:*

… whereto at midnight, the confessor came—a monk brown-robed and hooded—ghastly in the day and free bright air, but in the midnight of that murky prison Hope's extinguisher and Murder's herald …

The result of the second visit—he went in 1856 with his friend Wilkie Collins (q.v.)—was the section in the novel Little Dorrit *when the Dorrit family stays in Venice following the father's release from the Marshalsea debtors' prison. Mr Dorrit has surprisingly inherited great wealth and takes his family to Venice with a post-Grand Tour notion of acquiring gentility and social prestige by doing so.*

Little Dorrit (1857)
Charles Dickens

The family had been a month or two at Venice, when Mr Dorrit, who was much among Counts and Marquises, and had but scant leisure, set an hour of one day apart, beforehand, for the purpose of holding some conference with Mrs General.

The time he had reserved in his mind arriving, he sent Mr Tinkler, his valet, to Mrs General's apartment (which would have absorbed about a third of the area of the Marshalsea), to present his compliments to that lady, and represent him as desiring the favour of an interview. It being that period of the forenoon when the various members of the family had coffee in their own chambers, some couple of hours before assembling at breakfast in a faded hall which had once been sumptuous, but was now the prey of watery vapours and a settled melancholy, Mrs General was accessible to the valet. That envoy found her on a little square of carpet, so extremely diminutive in reference to the size of her stone and marble floor that she looked as if she might have had it spread for the trying on of a ready-made pair of shoes; or as if she had come into possession of the enchanted piece of carpet, bought for forty purses by one of the three princes in the Arabian Nights, and had that moment been transported on it, at a wish, into a palatial saloon with which it had no connection.

Mrs General, replying to the envoy, as she set down her empty coffee-cup, that she was willing at once to proceed to Mr Dorrit's apartment, and spare him the trouble of coming to her (which, in his gallantry, he had proposed), the envoy threw open the door, and escorted Mrs General to the presence. It quite was a walk, by mysterious staircases and corridors, from Mrs General's apartment,—hoodwinked by a narrow side street with a low gloomy bridge in it, and dungeon-like opposite tenements, their walls besmeared with a thousand downward stains and streaks, as if every crazy aperture in them had been weeping tears of rust into the Adriatic for centuries—to Mr Dorrit's apartment: with a whole English house-front of window, a prospect of beautiful church domes rising into the blue sky sheer out of the water which reflected them, and a hushed murmur of the Grand Canal laving the doorways below, where his gondolas and gondoliers attended his pleasure, drowsily swinging in a little forest of piles.

Mr Dorrit, in a resplendent dressing-gown and cap—the dormant grub that had so long bided its time among the Collegians [the debtors imprisoned in the Marshalsea] had burst into a rare butterfly—rose to receive Mrs General. A chair to Mrs General. An easier chair, sir; what are you doing, what are you about, what do you mean? Now, leave us!

'Mrs General,' said Mr Dorrit, 'I took the liberty—'

'By no means,' Mrs General interposed. 'I was quite at your disposition. I had had my coffee.'

'I took the liberty,' said Mr Dorrit again, with the magnificent placidity of one who was above correction, 'to solicit the favour of a little private conversation with you, because I feel rather worried respecting my—ha—my younger daughter. You will have observed a great difference of temperament, madam, between my two daughters?'

Said Mrs General in response, crossing her gloved hands (she was never without gloves, and they never creased and always fitted), 'There is a great difference.'

'May I ask to be favoured with your view of it?' said Mr Dorrit, with a deference not incompatible with majestic serenity.

'Fanny,' returned Mrs General, 'has force of character and self-reliance. Amy, none.' …

'But you are aware, my dear madam,' said Mr Dorrit, 'that my daughters had the misfortune to lose their lamented mother when they were very young; and that, in consequence of my not having been until lately the recognised heir to my property, they have lived with me as a comparatively poor, though always proud, gentleman, in—ha hum—retirement!'

'I do not,' said Mrs General, 'lose sight of the circumstance.'

'Madam,' pursued Mr Dorrit, 'of my daughter Fanny, under her present guidance and with such an example constantly before her—'

(Mrs General shut her eyes.)

'—I have no misgivings. There is adaptability of character in Fanny. But my younger daughter, Mrs General, rather worries and vexes my thoughts, I must inform you that she has always been my favourite.'

'There is no accounting,' said Mrs General, 'for these partialities.'

'Ha—no,' assented Mr Dorrit. 'No. Now, madam, I am troubled by noticing that Amy is not, so to speak, one of ourselves. She does not care to go about with us; she is lost in the society we have here; our tastes are evidently not her tastes. Which,' said Mr Dorrit, summing up with judicial gravity, 'is to say, in other words, that there is something wrong in—ha—Amy.'

'May we incline to the supposition,' said Mrs General, with a little touch of varnish, 'that something is referable to the novelty of the position?'

'Excuse me, madam,' observed Mr Dorrit, rather quickly. 'The daughter of a gentleman, though—ha—himself at one time comparatively far from affluent—comparatively—and herself reared in—hum—retirement, need not of necessity find this position so very novel.'

'True,' said Mrs General, 'true.'

'Therefore, madam,' said Mr Dorrit, 'I took the liberty' (he laid an emphasis on the phrase and repeated it, as though he stipulated, with urbane firmness, that he must not be contradicted again), 'I took the liberty of requesting this interview, in order that I might mention the topic to you, and inquire how you would advise me?'

'Mr Dorrit,' returned Mrs General, 'I have conversed with Amy several times since we have been residing here, on the general subject of the formation of a demeanour. She has expressed herself to me as wondering exceedingly at Venice. I have mentioned to her that it is better not to wonder. I have pointed out to her that the celebrated Mr Eustace, the classical tourist, did not think much of it; and that he compared the Rialto, greatly to its disadvantage, with Westminster and Blackfriars Bridges. I need not add, after what you have said, that I have not yet found my arguments successful. You do me the honour to ask me what to advise. It always appears to me (if this should prove to be a baseless assumption, I shall be pardoned), that Mr Dorrit has been accustomed to exercise influence over the minds of others.'

'Hum—madam,' said Mr Dorrit, 'I have been at the head of—ha—of a considerable community. You are right in supposing that I am not unaccustomed to—an influential position.'

'I am happy,' returned Mrs General, 'to be so corroborated. I would therefore the more confidently recommend that Mr Dorrit should speak to Amy himself, and make his observations and wishes known to her. Being his favourite, besides, and no doubt attached to him, she is all the more likely to yield to his influence.'

'I had anticipated your suggestion, madam,' said Mr Dorrit, 'but—ha—was not sure that I might—hum—not encroach on—'

'On my province, Mr Dorrit?' said Mrs General, graciously. 'Do not mention it.'

'Then, with your leave, madam,' resumed Mr Dorrit, ringing his little bell to summon his valet, 'I will send for her at once.'

'Does Mr Dorrit wish me to remain?'

'Perhaps, if you have no other engagement, you would not object for a minute or two—'

'Not at all.'

So, Tinkler the valet was instructed to find Miss Amy's maid, and to request that subordinate to inform Miss Amy that Mr Dorrit wished to see her in his own room. …

'Amy,' said Mr Dorrit, 'you have just now been the subject of some conversation between myself and Mrs General. We agree that you scarcely seem at home here. Ha—how is this?'

A pause.

'I think, father, I require a little time.'

'Papa is a preferable mode of address,' observed Mrs General.

'Father is rather vulgar, my dear. The word Papa, besides, gives a pretty form to the lips. Papa, potatoes, poultry, prunes, and prism are all very good words for the lips: especially prunes and prism. You will find it serviceable, in the formation of a demeanour, if you sometimes say to yourself in company—on entering a room, for instance—Papa, potatoes, poultry, prunes and prism, prunes and prism.'

'Pray, my child,' said Mr Dorrit, 'attend to the—hum—precepts of Mrs General.'

Poor Little Dorrit, with a rather forlorn glance at that eminent varnisher, promised to try.

'You say, Amy,' pursued Mr Dorrit, 'that you think you require time. Time for what?'

Another pause.

'To become accustomed to the novelty of my life, was all I meant,' said Little Dorrit, with her loving eyes upon her father; whom she had very nearly addressed as poultry, if not prunes and prism too, in her desire to submit herself to Mrs General and please him.

Mr Dorrit frowned, and looked anything but pleased. 'Amy,' he returned, 'it appears to me, I must say, that you have had abundance of time for that. Ha—you surprise me. You disappoint me. Fanny has conquered any such little difficulties, and—hum—why not you?'

'I hope I shall do better soon,' said Little Dorrit.

'I hope so,' returned her father. 'I—ha—I most devoutly hope so, Amy. I sent for you, in order that I might say—hum—impressively say, in the presence of Mrs General, to whom we are all so much indebted for obligingly being present among us, on—ha—on this or any other occasion,' Mrs General shut her eyes, 'that I—ha hum—am not pleased with you. You make Mrs General's a thankless task. You—ha—embarrass me very much. You have always (as I have informed Mrs General) been my favourite child; I have always made you a—hum—a friend and companion; in return, I beg—I —ha—I do beg, that you accommodate yourself better to—hum—circumstances, and dutifully do what becomes your—your station.'

Mr Dorrit was even a little more fragmentary than usual, being excited on the subject and anxious to make himself particularly emphatic.

'I do beg,' he repeated, 'that this may be attended to, and that you will seriously take pains and try to conduct yourself in a manner both becoming your position as—ha—Miss Amy Dorrit, and satisfactory to myself and Mrs General.'

That lady shut her eyes again, on being again referred to; then, slowly opening them and rising, added these words:

'If Miss Amy Dorrit will direct her own attention to, and will accept of my poor assistance in, the formation of a surface, Mr Dorrit will have no further cause of anxiety. May I take this opportunity of remarking, as an instance in point, that it is scarcely delicate to look at vagrants with the attention which I have seen bestowed upon them by a very dear young friend of mine? They should not be looked at. Nothing disagreeable should ever be looked at. Apart from such a habit standing in the way of that graceful equanimity of surface which is so expressive of good breeding, it hardly seems compatible with refinement of mind. A truly refined mind will seem to be ignorant of the existence of anything that is not perfectly proper, placid, and pleasant.' Having delivered this exalted sentiment, Mrs General made a sweeping obeisance, and retired with an expression of mouth indicative of Prunes and Prism.

First published as Little Dorrit, *Charles Dickens, Bradbury & Evans, 1857, following the serialisation in* Household Words, *Dec 1855–April 1857. Now widely available, for example* Little Dorrit, *Charles Dickens, Penguin, 2003.*

There are dozens of guide books to Venice. One of the most detailed is the Blue Guide *(by Alta Macadam), now in its ninth edition. The greatest 20th-century guides of the narrative* vade mecum *type are probably Hugh Honour's* Companion Guide to Venice *(see p. 104), J.G. Links's* Venice for Pleasure *(see p. 126), and* Venice on Foot *(1907), by Colonel Hugh A. Douglas.*

This last could be described as a compendium of Venice trivia—but that would make it sound trivial, which it certainly is not. Venice on Foot *is organised, as its title suggests, as a series of walks. Its detailed information and anecdote, combined with a good index, make it an excellent reference source as well as a pleasure to browse. 'If conscientiously followed,' as E.V. Lucas wrote in the preface to his own book on Venice in 1914, '[it] is such a key to a treasury of interest as no other city has ever possessed.' The original has long since disappeared from the shelves—even second-hand copies are almost impossible to find—but it is available to buy in various print-on-demand editions. This extract, describing the practice of organised pugilism on canal bridges, comes not from a walk, but from the General Notes at the end.*

Venice on Foot (1907)
Hugh A. Douglas

Guerra dei pugni (fight with fists). In the ninth century public fights with sticks used to take place in Venice between the men from Jesolo and the men from Eraclea, who were hereditary enemies. In the thirteenth century the Guerra dei Pugni, in which fists were used instead of sticks, took the place of the former. These were carried out between September and Christmas, on bridges built without parapets, so that the combatants might be thrown into the water, and be put *hors de combat* without being much hurt. These fights increased so in ferocity that in 1705, after a most sanguinary fight, at the close of which stones and knives were used, and many killed and injured, they were altogether forbidden, and the rivals had to content themselves with the 'Forze d'Ercole,' a species of gynmastic feat, which had also been in existence since the thirteenth century. It is not certain who were the first combatants in the Guerra dei Pugni, but from early in the fourteenth century they were the Castellani, who lived in the eastern part of the city, at the extremity of which was the island of Castello, and the Nicolotti, who inhabited the western part, at the extremity of which was the parish of San Nicolo dei Mendicoli. These two factions, who were deadly enemies, are thought by some to be the descendants of the people of Jesolo and Eraclea, but the enmity is generally supposed to have commenced in 1307, owing to the Nicolotti having killed a Bishop of Castello, who was quarrelling with the parish priest of San Pantalon about his death dues. The Republic are said to have encouraged the fights, and fostered the rivalry between these two factions; firstly, because the fighting served to render the men more plucky; and secondly, because the rivalry was a safeguard against revolution. This rivalry still shows itself, although not to the same extent as formerly, in the regattas that take place in the present day. A picture of the Guerra dei Pugni is to be seen in the picture gallery of the Palazzo Querini Stampaglia [sic.], and a bas-relief in bronze at the Museo Civico.

Venice on Foot, *Hugh A. Douglas, Methuen, 1907.*

ALBRECHT DÜRER

A man of great talent, dexterity and intellectual curiosity, Albrecht Dürer (1471–1528) was already famous by the time of his second visit to Venice in 1506. The son of a goldsmith who had emigrated from Hungary's Great Plain to Nuremburg, Dürer spent time in his 'gap year'—the Wanderjahr of a German apprentice—in the Netherlands and Alsace before his first visit to Venice in 1494. He was gifted with the ability

The familiar monogram 'AD' with which Dürer signed his pictures.

to imitate any artistic style, and his talents as a draughtsman were prodigious—the watercolour sketches he made of the Alps as he crossed them are acclaimed as the first natural landscapes in Western art. He also acted as a conduit of information between the Flemish and German schools in the north and Italy in the south. In Venice in particular he was much admired and, despite the professional jealousies of some local artists, much imitated.

As time went by he painted less, finding prints (woodcuts), in which he was highly skilled, more remunerative. In later life he was mainly occupied with his theoretical writing on subjects such as geometry (he called it 'measurement'), human proportions (including aesthetics) and fortifications. Following the example of Luther, whom he admired, he wrote not in Latin, which at that time was the lingua franca of scholarship, but in German.

By now prosperous from his art, he died at the age of 56, leaving a large house and workshop in Nuremburg, which still stands.

The extracts below are from letters from Venice to his close friend Wilibald Pirkheimer, a prominent Nuremburg lawyer and humanist scholar.

Records of Journeys to Venice and the Low Countries (1520/21)
Albrecht Dürer

Venice, 6th January 1506

My dear Master,

To you and all yours, many happy good New Years. My willing service to you, dear Herr Pirkheimer. Know that I am in good health; may God send you better even than that. Now as to what you commissioned me, namely, to buy a few pearls and precious stones, you must know that I can find nothing good enough or worth the money: everything is snapped up by the Germans.

Those who go about on the Riva always expect four times the value for anything, for they are the falsest knaves that live there. No one expects to get an honest service of them. For that reason some good people warned me to be on my guard against them. They told me that they cheat both man and beast, and that you could buy better things for less money at Frankfort than at Venice.

Venice, 7th February 1506

… How I wish you were here at Venice, there are so many good fellows among the Italians who seek my company more and more every day—which is very gratifying to me—men of sense, and scholarly, good lute-players, and pipers, connoisseurs in painting, men of much noble sentiment and honest virtue, and they show me much honour and friendship. On the other hand, there are also amongst them the most faithless, lying, thievish rascals; such as I scarcely believed could exist on earth; and yet if one did not know them, one would think that they were the nicest men on earth. I cannot help laughing to myself when they talk to me: they know that their villainy is well known, but that does not bother them.

I have many good friends among the Italians who warn me not to eat and drink with their painters, for many of them are my enemies and copy my work in the churches and wherever they can find it; afterwards they criticize it and claim that it is not done in the antique style and say it is no good, but Giambellin [Giovanni Bellini] has praised me highly to many gentlemen. He would willingly have something of mine, and came himself to me and asked me to do something for him, and said that he would pay well for it, and everyone tells me what an upright man he is, so that I am really friendly with him. He is very old and yet he is the best painter of all.

Venice, 28th February 1506

First my willing service to you, dear Herr Pirkheimer. If things go well with you, then I am indeed glad. Know, too, that by the grace of God I am doing well and working fast. Still I do not expect to have finished before Whitsuntide. I have sold all my pictures except one. For two I got 24 ducats, and the other three I gave for these three rings, which were valued in the exchange as worth 24 ducats, but I have shown them to some good friends and they say they are only worth 22, and as you wrote to me to buy you some jewels, I thought that I would send you the rings by Franz Imhof. Show them to people who understand them, and if you like them, keep them for what they are worth. In case you do not want them, send them back by the next messenger, for here at Venice a man who helped to make the exchange will give me 12 ducats for the emerald and 10 ducats for the ruby and diamond, so that I need not lose more than 2 ducats.

I wish you had occasion to come here, I know the time would pass quickly, for there are so many nice men here, real artists. And I have such a crowd of foreigners (Italians) about me that I am forced sometimes to shut myself up, and the gentlemen all wish me well, but few of the painters. …

Venice, 2nd April 1506

… The painters here you must know are very unfriendly to me. They have summoned me three times before the magistrates, and I have had to pay four florins to their School. You must know too that I might have gained much money if I had not undertaken to make the painting for the Germans, for there is a great deal of work in it and I cannot well finish it before Whitsuntide; yet they only pay me 85 ducats for it. [The 35 year-old Dürer had a keen appreciation of his own worth: the great Bellini, twice his age and one of Venice's most famous painters, would have expected about 100 ducats for a similar work.]

That, you know, will go in living expenses, and then I have bought some things, and have sent some money away, so that I have not much in hand now; but I have made up my mind not to leave here until God enables me to repay you with thanks and to have two florins over besides. I should easily earn this if I had not got to do the German picture, for, except the painters, everyone wishes me well…

Venice, 8th September 1506

…The Venetians are collecting many men; so is the Pope and the King of France. What will come of it I don't know, for people scoff at our King a great deal. [What came of it was the Venetian defeat at Agnadello in 1509.]

…My picture, you must know, says it would give a ducat for you to see it. It is well painted and finely coloured. I have got much praise but little profit by it. I could have easily earned 200 ducats in the time, and I have had to decline big commissions in order to come home.

I have shut up all the painters, who used to say that I was good at engraving, but that in painting I didn't know how to handle my colours. Now they all say they never saw better colouring. …

The Doge and the Patriarch have seen my picture. Herewith let me commend myself as your servant. I really must sleep, for it's striking seven at night, and I have already written to the Prior of the Augustines, to my father-in-law, to Mistress Dietrich, and to my wife, and they are all sheets cram full. So I have had to hurry over this. Read according to the sense. You would do it better if you were writing to princes. Many good nights to you, and days too. Given at Venice on Our Lady's Day in September.

Venice, 23rd September 1506

Your letter telling me of the overflowing praise that you received from princes and nobles gave me great *allegrezza* [joy]. You must have changed completely to have become so gentle; I must do likewise when I meet you again. Know also that my picture is finished, likewise another quadro, the like of which I never made before. And as you are so pleased with yourself, let me tell you now that there is no better Madonna picture in all the land, for all the painters praise it as the nobles do you. They say that they have never seen a nobler, more charming painting.

The oil for which you wrote I am sending by Kannengiesser. And burnt glass that I sent you by Farber—tell me if it reached you safely. As for the carpets, I have not bought any yet, for I cannot find any square ones. They are all narrow and long. If you would like any of these, I will willingly buy them; let me know about it.

Know also that in four weeks at the latest I shall be finished here, for I have to paint first some portraits that I have promised, and in order that I may get home soon, I have refused, since my picture was finished, orders for more than 2,000 ducats; all my neighbours know of this. …

The Humanist's Library, *Vol. VI, edited by Lewis Einstein, translated by Rudolf Tombo, The Merrymount Press: Boston, 1913.*

GEORGE ELIOT

In the early 1860s, Mary Ann Evans (1819–80), who published her novels under the name George Eliot, visited Italy at least three times in the company of her de facto husband, George Lewes. She was subsequently to spend a lot of time travelling in Europe—also in Germany, Spain and France—assiduously visiting galleries and museums, thinking earnestly about the art she saw and noting her impressions in her journals. Much of this material was later used in her novels—notably in Romola *(set in 15th-century Florence), but also, in passing, in* Middlemarch *and* Daniel Deronda. *In 1880 she returned with her second (much younger) husband, John Walter Cross: during their honeymoon in Venice, Cross purportedly jumped or fell from the balcony of their room into the Grand Canal—and survived.*

The account below dates from Eliot's first visit to Venice in 1860, undertaken as part of a 'grand Italian tour'. The spirit of almost childlike excitement with which she describes her arrival in Venice contrasts markedly with the oppressive feelings of her greatest fictional character, Dorothea Casaubon in Middlemarch *(Chapter 20), on her first visit to Rome. Indeed George Eliot writes with such breathless speed about the visit that she hardly gives herself time to reflect on what she sees. It is only in the journal of a subsequent journey to Venice in 1864 that she writes in detail about the paintings which she saw in the city—Titian's* Annunciation, *or Palma Vecchio's magnificent* St Barbara, *which struck her as 'an almost unique presentation of a hero-woman … filled with serious conviction'—perhaps a resemblance of her own image of herself.*

The tenebrous interior of St Mark's appears not to have appealed to Eliot's Victorian sensibility. She seems instead to revel in the simple joy of the novelty of Venice. As such, the passage reveals a spontaneous and less well-known side to the great novelist's thoughtful personality.

Letters and Journals (1860–80)
George Eliot

[1860]

From Padua to Venice! It was about ten o'clock on a moonlight night—the 4th of June—that we found ourselves apparently on a railway in the midst of the sea: we were on the bridge across the lagoon. Soon we were in a gondola on the Grand Canal, looking out at the moonlit buildings and water. What stillness! What beauty! Looking out from the high window of our hotel on the Grand Canal, I felt that it was a pity to go to bed. Venice was more beautiful than romances had feigned.

And that was the impression that remained, and even deepened, during our stay of eight days. That quiet which seems the deeper because one hears the delicious dip of the oar (when not disturbed by clamorous church bells), leaves the eye in full liberty and strength to take in the exhaustless loveliness of colour and form.

We were in our gondola by nine o'clock the next morning, and of course the first point we sought was the Piazza di San Marco. I am glad to find Ruskin calling the Palace of the Doges one of the two most perfect buildings in the world. … This spot is a focus of architectural wonders: but the palace is the crown of them all. The double tier of columns and arches, with the rich sombreness of their finely outlined shadows, contrast satisfactorily with the warmth and light and more continuous surface of the upper part. Even landing on the Piazzetta, one has a sense, not only of being in an entirely novel scene, but one where the ideas of a foreign race have poured themselves in without yet mingling indistinguishably with the pre-existent Italian life. But this is felt yet more strongly when one has passed along the Piazzetta and arrived in front of San Marco, with its low arches and domes and minarets. But perhaps the most striking point to take one's stand on is just in front of the white marble guard-house flanking the great tower—the guard-house with Sansovino's iron gates before it. On the left is San Marco, with the two square pillars from St. Jean d'Acre, standing as isolated trophies; on the right the Piazzetta extends between the Doge's palace and the Palazzo Reale to the tall columns from Constantinople; and in front is the elaborate gateway leading to the white marble Scala dei Giganti, in the courtyard of the Doge's palace. Passing through this gateway and up the staircase, we entered the gallery which surrounds the court on three sides, and looked down at the fine sculptured vase-like wells below. Then into the great Sala, surrounded with the portraits of the Doges: the largest oil-painting here—or perhaps anywhere else— is the '*Gloria del Paradiso*' by Tintoretto, now dark and unlovely. But on the ceiling is a great Paul Veronese—the '*Apotheosis of Venice*'—which looks as fresh as if it were painted yesterday, and is a miracle of colour and composition—a picture full of glory and joy of an earthly, fleshly kind, but without any touch of coarseness or vulgarity. Below the radiant Venice on her clouds is a balcony filled with upward-looking spectators; and below this gallery is a group of human figures with horses. Next to this *Apotheosis*, I admire another *Coronation of Venice* on the ceiling of another Sala, where Venice is sitting enthroned above the globe with her lovely face in half-shadow—a creature born with an imperial attitude. There are other Tintorettos, Veroneses, and Palmas in the great halls of this palace; but they left me quite indifferent, and have become vague in my memory. From the splendours of the palace we crossed the Bridge of Sighs to the prisons, and saw the horrible dark damp cells that would make the saddest life in the free light and air seem bright and desirable.

The interior of St. Mark's is full of interest, but not of beauty: it is dark and heavy, and ill-suited to the Catholic worship, for the massive piers that obstruct the view everywhere shut out the sight of ceremony and procession, as we witnessed at our leisure on the day of the great procession of Corpus Christi. But everywhere there are relics of gone-by art to be studied, from mosaics of the Greeks to mosaics of later artists than the Zuccati [the Zuccati were active in the 16th-century]; old marble statues, embrowned like a meerschaum pipe; amazing sculptures in wood; Sansovino doors, ambitious to rival Ghiberti's; transparent alabaster columns; an ancient Madonna, hung with jewels, transported from St. Sophia, in Constantinople; and everywhere the venerable pavement, once beautiful with its starry patterns in rich marble, now deadened and sunk to unevenness like the mud floor of a cabin. Then outside, on the archway of the principal door, there are sculptures of a variety that makes one renounce the study of them in despair at the shortness of one's time—blended fruits and foliage, and human groups and animal forms of all kinds. On our first morning we ascended the great tower, and looked around on the island-city and the distant mountains and the distant Adriatic. And on the same day we went to see the Pisani Palace—one of the grand old palaces that are going to decay. … After this we saw the Church of San Sebastiano, where Paul Veronese is buried, with his own paintings around, mingling their colour with the light that falls on his tombstone. There is one remarkably fine painting of his here: it represents, I think, some Saints going to martyrdom, but apart from that explanation, is a composition full of vigorous, spirited figures.

Letters and Journals, *George Eliot*, edited by J.W. Cross, *Harper, 1885.*

JOHN EVELYN

John Evelyn (1620–1706) was a horticulturalist, hospital administrator, clean-air campaigner and —most famously—a diarist, with a vast and untrammelled intellectual curiosity. The prolix impersonality of his diaries is often compared unfavourably with the vitality of his friend Samuel Pepys's famous account of life in London in the 1660s. In the 1640s, finding Civil-War England uncongenial, and being easily discouraged from enrolling in the Royalist Army, Evelyn travelled extensively in continental Europe, including Venice. It was only 50 years later, after a distinguished life of public service (which included founder-membership of the Royal Society and authorship of its first publication: Sylva, or A Discourse on Forest-Trees and the Propagation of Timber in His Majesty's Dominions), that he wrote up his diaries of those travels.

These two extracts are taken from Alfred H. Hyatt's The Charm of Venice, an anthology as charming as the title suggests of brief literary and historical extracts about Venice, published in 1908. Details are given in the short bibliography on p. 218.

Diary (covering the years 1657–88)
John Evelyn

On the Carnival

All the world repaire to Venice to see the folly and madnesse of the Carnevall; the women, men, and persons of all conditions disguising themselves in antiq dresses, with extravagant musiq and a thousand gambols, traversing the streetes from house to house, all places being there accessible and free to enter. Abroad, they fling eggs fill'd with sweete water. ...The youth of the severall wards and parishes contend in other masteries and pastimes, so that 'tis impossible to recount the universal madnesse of this place during this time of licence. The greate banks are set up for those who will play bassett [a card game]; the comedians have liberty, and the operas are open; witty pasquils [lampoons] are thrown about, and the mountebanks have their stages at every corner.

On Venetian Dames

It was now Ascension Weeke, and the greate Marte of Faire of the whole yeare was now kept, every body at liberty and jollie. The noblemen stalking with their ladys on choppines; these are high-heel'd shoes, particularly affected by these proude dames, or, as some may say, invented to keepe them at home, it being very difficult to walke with them; whence one being asked how he liked the Venetian dames, replied that they were *mezzo carne, mezzo ligno*, half flesh, half wood, and he would have none of them. The truth is, their garb is very odd, as seeming all wayes in masquerade; their other habits are also totally different from all nations. They weare long crisped haire, of severall strakes and colours, which they make so by a wash, dishevelling it on the brims of a broade hat that has no head, but an hole to put out their heads by; they drie them in the sunne, as one may see them at their windows. In their tire they set silk flowers and sparkling stones, their peticotes coming from their very arme-pits, so that they are neere three-quarters and an half apron; their sleeves are made exceedingly wide...and commonly tucked up to the shoulder, showing their naked armes, thro' false sleeves of tiffany, girt with a bracelet or two, with knots of points richly tagged about their shoulders and other places of their body, which they usually cover with a kind of yellow vaile of lawn very transparent. Thus attir'd they set their hands on the heads of two matron-like servants or old women, to support them, who are mumbling their beades. 'Tis ridiculous to see how these ladys crawle in and out of their gondolas by reason of their choppines, and what dwarfs they appeare when taken downe from their wooden scaffolds; of these I saw nearly thirty together, stalking half as high again as the rest of the world, for courtezans or the citizens may not weare chop-pines, but cover their bodies and faces with a vaile of a certaine glittering taffeta or lustree, out of which they now and then dart a glaunce of their eye, the whole face being otherwise entirely hid with it; nor may the common misses take this habit, but go abroad bare-fac'd. To the corners of these virgin-vailes hang broad but flat tossells of curious Point de Venize; the married women go in black vailes. The nobility weare the same colour, but of fine cloth lin'd with taffeta in summer, and fur of the bellies of squirrels in the winter, which all put on at a certaine day girt with a girdle emboss'd with silver; the vest not much different from what our Bachelors of Arts weare in Oxford, and a hood of cloth made like a sack, cast over their left shoulder, and a round cloth black cap fring'd with wool which is not so comely; they also weare their collar open to shew the diamond buttons of the stock of their shirt. I have never seene pearles for colour and bignesse comparable to what the lady's wear, most of the noble families being very rich in jewells, especially pearles.

Extracts from John Evelyn's Diary *taken from* The Charm of Venice, *Alfred H. Hyatt, Chatto & Windus, 1908. The* Diary *was first published in the* Memoirs of John Evelyn, *comprising his diary from 1641 to 1705–06 and a selection of his familiar letters edited by William Bray, Frederick Warne and Co., 1818. More recently John Evelyn's* Diary *has been published in full in* The Writings of John Evelyn, *edited by Guy de la Bédoyère, Boydell and Brewer, Woodbridge, 1995.*

GOETHE

Johann Wolfgang von Goethe's (1749–1842) first departure for Italy has all the elements of an elopement. Unannounced to his friends, at three o'clock in the morning and under a false name, the 37-year-old poet abandoned both his position as a functionary of the State of Weimar and his companion and confidant of many years, Charlotte von Stein, and set off in full haste for Italy. 'The com-pelling desire to see this country had too long been maturing within me', he wrote not long after his ar-rival. He saw the architecture of the

Etching from the book *Portrait Gallery of Eminent Men and Women in Europe and America*, published in 1873.

ancient world for the first time in his life at the Arena in Verona, and had his first sight of the sea in Venice. His visits to Italy over the next two years were to transform his poetry and his thinking. In Italy he found what his spirit craved—the exact opposite of the world of Wei-mar which he had left behind. Italy was rich in colour, where Germany was grey; it was spontaneous, as opposed to controlled; it was pagan, ancient, luminous, liberating, passionate—all those things that his re-spectable life as an administrator and his platonic relationship with Charlotte von Stein were not. His Italian visits inaugurate a long series of intellectual love-affairs between the northern European mind and the Italian spirit. Many artists were to follow in Goethe's steps over the next two centuries; though few expressed their thoughts and sentiments with such calm profundity.

Goethe arrived in Venice on 28th September 1786 and stayed in the city a little over two weeks. He observed and visited assiduously, filling his time with looking at architecture, observing customs and go-ing frequently to the theatre. Almost every day in his journal he wrote interestingly about what he saw. The tone is light and youthful: above all, it gives a clear sense of a brilliant, humane and thoroughly sym-

pathetic personality. His entries for the 6th and 7th October cover a typical diversity of subjects: thoughts on a tragedy by Gozzi seen the previous evening; observations on Palladio; a painterly description of an annual Venetian ceremony commemorating the victory of Lepanto; and a wonderful account of the antiphonal singing of the Venetian gondoliers across the silent, nocturnal spaces of the city—something which was also to captivate Wagner (see p. 209) when he lived in Venice 80 years later.

Italian Journey (1786–88)
Johann Wolfgang von Goethe

6th October [1786]

I learned many things from yesterday's tragedy [a production by Carlo Gozzi]. To begin with, I heard how the Italians declaim their iambic hendecasyllabics. Then I now see with what skill Gozzi combined the use of masks with tragic characters. This is the proper spectacle for a people who want to be moved in the crudest way. They take no sentimental interest in misfortune and enjoy themselves only if the hero declaims well. They set great store by rhetoric and, at the same time, they want to laugh at some nonsense.

Their interest in a play is limited to what they feel is real. When the tyrant handed his son a sword and ordered him to kill his own wife, who was standing before him, the public expressed its displeasure at such an unreasonable demand, and so noisily that they almost stopped the play. They yelled at the old man to take his sword back, an action which would, of course, have wrecked the subsequent situations in the play. In the end, the harassed son came down to the footlights and humbly implored the audience to be patient for a little because the business would certainly conclude exactly as they hoped. But, artistically speaking, the situation of which the public complained was absurd and unnatural, and I heartily approved of their feelings.

I now understood better the long speeches and the many passages of dialectic in Greek tragedy. The Athenians were even fonder of talking than the Italians, besides being better at it. Their dramatists must certainly have learned something at the tribunals, where they spent whole days.

Looking at the buildings which Palladio completed, in particular at his churches, I have found much to criticize side by side with great excellence. While I was asking myself how far I was right or wrong about this extraordinary man, he seemed to be standing beside me, saying: 'This or that I did against my will, nevertheless I did it because it was the closest approximation to my ideal possible under the circumstances.'

The more I think about him, the more strongly I feel that, when he looked at the height and width of an old church or house for which he had to make a new façade, he must have said to himself: 'How can you give this building the noblest form possible? Because of contradictory demands, you are bound to bungle things here and there, and it may well happen that there will be same incongruities. But the building as a whole will be in a noble style, and you will enjoy doing the work.' It was in this way that he executed the great conception he had in mind, even when it was not quite suitable and he had to mangle it in the details.

The wing of the Carità, therefore, must be doubly precious to us because here the artist was given a free hand and could obey his genius unconditionally. Had the convent been finished, there would probably be no more perfect work of architecture in the whole world today. [It is now incorporated into the Accademia Galleries.]

The more I read his writings and note as I do his treatment of Classical antiquity, the more clearly I understand how he thought and worked. He was a man of few words, but every one of them carries weight. As a study of Classical temples, his fourth volume is an excellent introduction for the intelligent reader.

7th October [1786]

…For this evening I had made arrangements to hear the famous singing of the boatmen, who chant verses by Tasso and Ariosto to their own melodies. This performance has to be ordered in advance, for it is now rarely done and belongs, rather, to the half-forgotten legends of the past. The moon had risen when I took my seat in a gondola and the two singers, one in the prow, the other in the stern, began chanting verse after verse in turns. The melody, which we know from Rousseau, is something between chorale and recitative. It always moves at the same tempo without any definite beat. The modulation is of the same character; the singers change pitch according to the content of the verse in a kind of declamation.

I shall not go into the question of how the melody evolved. It is enough to say that it is ideal for someone idly singing to himself and adapting the tune to poems he knows by heart. The singer sits on the shore of an island, on the bank of a canal or in a gondola, and sings at the top of his voice—the people here appreciate volume more than anything else. His aim is to make his voice carry as far as possible over the still mirror of water. Far away another singer hears it. He knows the melody and the words and answers with the next verse. The first singer answers again, and so on. Each is the echo of the other. They keep this up night after night without ever getting tired. If the listener has chosen the right spot, which is halfway between them, the further apart they are, the more enchanting the singing will sound.

To demonstrate this, my boatmen tied up the gondola on the shore of the Giudecca and walked along the canal in opposite directions. I walked back and forth, leaving the one, who was just about to sing, and walking towards the other, who had just stopped. For the first time I felt the full effect of this singing. The sound of their voices far away was extraordinary, a lament without sadness, and I was moved to tears. I put this down to my mood at the moment, but my old manservant said: '*è singolare, come quel canto intenerisce, e molto più, quando e più ben cantato.'* [It is interesting how poignant this singing is, the more so when well sung.] He wanted me to hear the women on the Lido, especially those from Malamocco and Pellestrina. They too, he told me, sing verses by Tasso to the same or a similar melody, and added: 'It is their custom to sit on the seashore while their husbands are out sea-fishing, and sing these songs in penetrating tones until, from far out over the sea, their men reply, and in this way they converse with each other.' Is this not a beautiful custom? I dare say that, to someone standing close by, the sound of such voices competing with the thunder of the waves, might not be very agreeable. But the motive behind such singing is so human and genuine that it makes the mere notes of the melody, over which scholars have racked their brains in vain, come to life. It is the cry of some lonely human being sent out into the wide world till it reaches the ears of another lonely human being who is moved to answer it.

Italian Journey, *Johann Wolfgang von Goethe, 1816. This version translated by W.H. Auden and Elizabeth Mayer, Collins, 1962. Copyright © 1962 by W.H. Auden and Elizabeth Mayer. Reprinted by permission of Curtis Brown, Ltd.*

PEGGY GUGGENHEIM

Peggy Guggenheim on the steps of the Greek Pavilion, where she exhibited her collection at the 24th Venice Biennale, with *Interior* (1945, unknown location) by her daughter Pegeen Vail; 1948.

Peggy Guggenheim (1898–1979), restless heiress and prescient collector of modern art, moved to Venice in 1946 after a turbulent life in New York, Paris and London, with spells almost everywhere else fashionable in Europe ('Berlin was horrible… I walked all over the city and saw nothing to justify my curiosity. We went to the opera and some night clubs full of gay boys but it was all very dreary'). A constant refrain in her autobiography, spoken or unspoken, was 'But of course we got restless and decided to travel again'. During the 1920s and 30s and even in the war years she partied with, collected, exhibited or otherwise supported financially many painters and sculptors later to be famous such as Brancusi, Duchamp, Cocteau, Kandinsky, Jackson Pollock, Arp, Rothko and Giacometti. Guggenheim married twice, each time to an artist. Her first husband was the Dadaist Laurence Vail (with whom she had two children) and her second the Surrealist Max Ernst.

For most of the last 30 years of her life she lived in Venice, working on her collection. A niece of Solomon Guggenheim—her own father Benjamin had drowned on the Titanic—she was delighted in 1969 to be asked to leave her collection to the Solomon R. Guggenheim Foundation, which she duly did. The museum in what became her Venice home, the unfinished Palazzo Venier on the Grand Canal, is now administered together with the Guggenheim Museum in New York as well as with its new satellite museums in Berlin, Bilbao and Abu Dhabi.

Here, in extracts from her breathless but very readable autobiography Out of this Century: Confessions of an Art Addict, *she describes her life in Venice, relatively tranquil after the non-stop party that had occupied much of her time between the wars.*

Out of This Century: Confessions of an Art Addict (1946–79)
Peggy Guggenheim

It was through Santomaso [an artist she met in a café] that I was invited to show my entire collection at the XXIVth Biennale of Venice. He had suggested to Rodolfo Pallucchini, the secretary-general of the Biennale, that the collection should be exhibited, and it was agreed that it should be shown in the Greek pavilion, which was free because of the Greeks being at war.

The Biennale, which started in 1895, is an international exhibition of contemporary art, which is held every other year in the Public Gardens at the end of Venice, on the lagoon near the Lido. A lot of very ugly buildings put up in the time of Mussolini give it a distinct character. The trees and the gardens are wonderfully looked after and make a beautiful background for the various pavilions. In the middle of June, when the Biennale opens, the lime trees are flowering and the perfume they exhale is overpowering. I often feel this must compete strongly with the exhibition, as it is so much pleasanter to sit in the gardens than to go into the terribly hot and unventilated pavilions. …

In 1948, after so many years of disuse, the pavilions were in a bad state and there was an awful lot of repairing going on up to the last minute. My pavilion was being done over by Scarpa, who was the most modern architect in Venice. Pallucchini, the secretary-general, was not at all conversant with modern art. He was a great student of the Italian Renaissance, and it must have been difficult for him, as well as very brave, to do his task. When he gave a lecture in my pavilion he asked me to help him distinguish the various schools; he was even unfamiliar with the painters. Unfortunately I had to go to the dentist, but he claimed that he had managed without me. …

In 1948 the foreign pavilions were, naturally, à la page. But some were still very much behind the Iron Curtain. I was allowed to hang my collection three days before the Biennale opened. Actually, I wanted to go to Ravenna with Dr. Sandberg, the director of the Stedelijk Museum in Amsterdam, who had already finished his work in the Dutch pavilion. But this was out of the question, so I buckled down to work. Fortunately I was given a free hand and a lot of efficient workmen, who did not mind my perpetual changes. We managed to get the show finished in time, and though it was terribly crowded it looked gay and attractive, all on white walls—so different from Kiesler's decor for Art of This Century.

The opening of the Biennale was very formal, but, as usual, I had no hat, stockings or gloves and was in quite a dilemma. I borrowed stocking and a girdle from a friend, and instead of a hat wore enormous marguerite-flowered earrings made out of Venetian glass beads. Count Elio Zorzi, the head of the press office and the ambassador of the Biennale, who had actually extended to me the Biennale invitation, gave me strict instructions that when President Einaudi came to my pavilion I should try to explain to him as much as I could about modern art in the five minutes he would remain with me. I received exactly contrary orders from Pallucchini, who said the president was lame and would be terribly tired after visiting the whole Biennale, my pavilion being his last effort.

When His Excellency arrived he greeted me by saying, 'Where is your collection?' I said, 'Here,' and he corrected himself and asked where it had been before. I tried to obey Count Zorzi rather than Pallucchini, and put in a few words, but luckily the photographers intervened and the entire official party was photographed with Gonella, the minister of education, the president and me under my lovely Calder mobile.

The same morning I had a visit from the American ambassador and the consular staff. The United States pavilion was not open, as the pictures had not arrived in time, and James Dunn, our ambassador, was very pleased that at least I represented the United States. Looking at one of my abstract Picassos, he seemed rather happy to note that it was 'almost normal.' …

The two most unfortunate things that occurred at the Biennale were the theft of a little piece of bronze from a David Hare sculpture representing a baby; it must have been taken as a souvenir. And the other was Pallucchini's decision (as some priests were coming to visit my pavilion) to take down a very sexual Matta drawing of centaurs and nymphs. The drawing itself was so annoyed that it fell on the ground and the glass broke into smithereens, thus obviating its insulting removal.

A third catastrophe was avoided by Bruno Alfieri, who saved a dismantled Calder mobile from being thrown away by the workmen, who thought that it was bits of iron bands which had come off the packing cases.

My exhibition had enormous publicity and the pavilion was one of the most popular of the Biennale. I was terribly excited by all this, but what I enjoyed most was seeing the name of Guggenheim appearing on the maps in the Public Gardens next to the names of Great Britain, France, Holland, Austria, Switzerland, Poland, Palestine, Denmark, Belgium, Egypt, Czechoslovakia, Hungary, Romania. I felt as though I were a new European country.

My next illustrious visitor was Bernard Berenson. I greeted him as he came up my steps and told him how much I had studied his books and how much they had meant to me. His reply was, 'Then why do you go in for this?' I knew beforehand how much he hated modern art and said, 'I couldn't afford old masters, and anyhow I consider it one's duty to protect the art of one's time.' He replied 'you should have come to me, my dear, I would have found you bargains.' He liked best the works of Max Ernst and Pollock. Nevertheless, he said Max's were too sexual and that he did not like sex in art; the Pollocks, to him, were like tapestries. He was horrified by a little bronze Moore, a reclining figure of a woman, which he said was distorted. …

I used to go myself to the Biennale every few days and take my dogs with me. They were very well treated by a restaurant at the entrance called the Paradiso, and always given ice cream on their way in. Therefore whenever I asked them if they wished to accompany me to the Biennale, they wagged their tails and jumped with joy. They were the only dogs admitted to the exhibition, and when they were lost in this labyrinth I always found them in the Picasso exhibition; which proves how valuable their education had been at Art of This Century, where they had accompanied me every day.

In the autumn of 1949, I made an exhibition of more or less recent sculpture in the garden, and Professor Giuseppe Marchiori, a well-known critic, wrote the introduction to the catalogue. We exhibited an Arp, a Brancusi, a Calder mobile, three Giacomettis, a Lipchitz, a Moore, a Pevsner, a David Hare, from my collection, and a Mirko, a Consagra, a Salvatore and two Vianis, which we borrowed from the artists. There was also a Marino Marini, which I bought from him in Milan. I went to borrow one for the sculpture show, but ended up by buying the only thing available. It was a statue of a horse and rider, the latter with his arms spread way out in ecstasy, and to emphasize this, Marini had added a phallus in full erection. But when he had it cast in bronze for me he had the phallus made separately, so that it could be screwed in and out at leisure. Marini placed the sculpture in my courtyard on the Grand Canal, opposite the Prefettura, and named it *The Angel of the Citadel*. Herbert Read said the statue was a challenge to the prefect. The best view of it was to be seen in profile from my sitting room window. Often, peeking through it, I watched the visitors' reaction to the statue.

When the nuns came to be blessed by the Patriarch, who on special holy days, went by my house in a motorboat, I detached the phallus of the horseman and hid it in a drawer. I also did this on certain days when I had to receive stuffy visitors, but occasionally I forgot, and when confronted with this phallus found myself in great embarrassment. The only thing to do in such cases was to ignore it. In Venice a legend spread that I had several phalluses of different sizes, like spare parts, which I used on different occasions.

Apart from this [sponsoring two Italian painters, Tancredi and Edmondo Bacci], and opening my house to the public three afternoons a week, I have not done much in Italy. Santomaso was madly disappointed, as he thought I was about to become a new dynamic and cultural center for Italian art. But I was so uninspired by what I found in Italy that little by little I lost interest. The painting in the Biennale gets worse every year. Everybody just copies the people who did interesting things forty years ago, and so it goes on down the line, getting more and more stereotyped and more and more boring. I have continued buying whenever possible, but infinitely prefer contemporary sculpture to painting.

Since my collection has been opened to the public, people come from all over the world to see it, and as I also hold a salon for intellectuals, a great confusion arises. Anyone is welcome to visit the gallery on public days, but some people, not understanding this, think that I should be included as a sight. I get phone calls from many persons whom I do not know, who begin by saying, 'You don't know me, but I once met your sister Hazel in California.' or 'Your friend Paul Bowles told me to phone you,' or 'We have just arrived in Venice and have a letter of introduction to you, and would like to invite you to lunch or dinner or a drink.' On one occasion a young American, in Italy on a Guggenheim musical fellowship, even wrote and asked if I had a piano, as he would like to come and practice on it. I was happy to be able to say I hadn't got one. I would never dare phone a stranger on such flimsy pretenses. If I had a letter of introduction, I would send it round and wait to be invited. People don't know how to behave any more. Oh, for the good old days, when they still had manners!

© Out of this Century: Confessions of an Art Addict, *Peggy Guggenheim, André Deutsch, 2005.*

L.P. HARTLEY

L.P. Hartley (1895–1972) wrote stories in which the protagonist is strangely detached from, sometimes traumatised by, the goings on of a grown-up, generally upper-class, Edwardian world. He is best known for The Go-Between, which was published in 1953 and which opens with the famous line 'The past is another country, they do things differently there'. The 1971 film was based on an adaptation by Harold Pinter and starred Alan Bates and Julie Christie.

Venice became a necessity for the sensitive Hartley, who spent several months a year there between the two wars, mixing with its foreign and local high society. Much of Eustace and Hilda *(1947), the last in his* Shrimp and the Anemone *trilogy, is set in the city, where the young novelist-in-the-making Eustace enjoys the escape from a suffocating family and his competent, worldly elder sister Hilda. He is taken up by the society hostess Lady Nelly, and on the festival of the Feast of the Redeemer joins the crowds who go to swim on the Lido beach at dawn. Lady Nelly's private gondola is no longer there by the time he decides to return, and he is offered a lift back to Venice by a Venetian family in their small boat.*

Eustace and Hilda (1944)
L.P. Hartley

Though there was very little wind there was a good deal of motion on the water, and Eustace, tired and empty, soon began to feel it. He stole a look at the other passengers to see how much sympathy he might expect from them should he be sea-sick. The mother was bending over her child. It stirred fretfully and cried, and the older woman made as though to take it from her, but she resisted and their eyes clashed almost angrily. The old man was leaning on his elbow sucking a cigarette, and occasionally spitting; the young man stared ahead of him. They were all absorbed in their own concerns. Warning signals flashed along Eustace's exhausted nerves. They were passing the Armenian monastery; he would fix his mind on that, and on Byron who had surely never been sea-sick when he rowed out there to write. But somehow the monastery seemed a building like any other, and its pink walls, that reminded him of blotting-paper, were no antidote to a queasy stomach. But with his eyes unoccupied, his stomach certainly fared worse; he would hold out till he got to the next landmark, the island monastery of San Servolo. How cleverly the architect had adapted his design to the shape of the island! But the biscuit-coloured walls were lustreless, the windows monotonously regular and sometimes barred: Eustace's eye slid along them without finding relief. The boatman stopped rowing and stretched out his hand towards the building.

'Manicomio,' he remarked with a smile of amusement.

'Pazzi,' he added, when Eustace showed no sign of understanding. Seeing that Eustace was still in the dark, he made the international gesture of tapping his forehead. The decorative island of San Servolo was a lunatic asylum.

The discovery increased Eustace's malaise, and he looked round desperately for some new object on which to concentrate. There were a great many to choose from, for he was now riding the waters of the Bacino in the heart of picturesque Venice—the extremely agitated waters, and it behoved him to act quickly. But all the buildings were so off colour he did not know which to look at—literally off colour, for under the hard, thick glare the pinks and greys, scarcely distinguishable from each other, had the same monotonous message for his mind. The sighings and subsidings within him grew more imperative and told him his time was short. The rose-brown campanile of San Giorgio Maggiore was as dumb as the shut, pallid face of the church it guarded. From the great blank oblong of the Doge's palace the pink lozenges had faded altogether. A colourless Venice! Fortune's ball, topping the Dogana, looked a tedious nought, an empty O, a mere dull round, robbed of its gold-green patina. Nothing could injure the shape of the Salute, but even it seemed less impressive, a uniform lifeless grey, a few tones darker than the sky, but made of the same substance.

And how must he appear, thought Eustace suddenly, to all these glorious buildings, the delight and despair of Guardi, Canaletto, Marieschi, Turner, Sargent, and how many more? What must they think of this poor creature huddled in his overcoat, tossing up and down in a dirty little black boat, his unshaven face green with nausea, his companions the refuse of the Venetian populace?

Desperately he looked for comfort outside the charmed circle of architectural aristocrats. As sickly as the rest of him, his eyes travelled slowly across the heaving water of the Giudecca Canal and rested on the austere geometry of the Redentore Church. He had forgotten it. It still drew his eyes with its mysterious apartness, its proud isolation. Eustace fancied that unlike the circle of notables it had not suffered a sea-change, it had not shed its glory of the night before. The controlled strength and the call to discipline in that stern regard were just the tonic he needed.

Drawing a less hazardous breath he instinctively turned round. But the dews of sickness had come out on his brow and his companion in the boat imagined him worse than he was. Far from being horrified or shocked they were all sympathy. Cries of 'Ahi, poveretto!' rang out; even the baby roused itself and smiled at him as if this was something it thoroughly understood. Silencing a buzz of advice and counter-advice the young man, to Eustace's dismay, held his forehead with one hand while with the other he pressed to his lips a flagon of red wine that had been conjured out of the bottom of the boat. The wine was sour and rough, but most reviving. By the time they reached the Piazzetta, Eustace was feeling nearly well. Only in body, however. His spirits had again sunk to zero. He had remembered to bring so many things for the expedition: a book in case he should be bored, two handkerchiefs in case he lost one, a bottle of aspirin, and of course his brandy-flask, which he had forgotten to use. But no money. He was so used to being paid for he had forgotten to bring any. Until the young man gave him the wine, the question of payment had not occurred to Eustace. But it must have occurred to the young man; indeed, it must have been his reason for offering Eustace the lift.

Eustace rehearsed the sentences which were to make his position clear—the shame he felt, the kindness he could never acknowledge, the rich reward waiting at the Palazzo Sfortunato. But hardly had he begun, 'Scusi, signore—,' when the young man, backed up by all his relations, passionately disclaimed any wish to be repaid. He smiled; they all smiled; they diffused the dignity and reserve of people whose lives are spent in bestowing unrequited favours; they seemed to be, for the first time that morning, enjoying themselves. Nothing had been a trouble, everything had been a pleasure, might they all soon meet again.

Eustace and Hilda, L.P. Hartley, Faber & Faber Ltd, 1975. Reproduced with kind permission of The Society of Authors as the literary representative of the estate of L.P. Hartley.

HUGH HONOUR

The Companion Guide to Venice *by Hugh Honour (b. 1927) is one of the finest 20th-century guide books to the city. It is part of the still extant famous* Companion Guide *series, and like two other great Venice guide books, J.G. Links's* Venice for Pleasure *(see p. 126) and Hugh A. Douglas's* Venice on Foot *(see p. 75), it is arranged as a series of walks. As the name 'companion' guide is intended to imply, the author is given space for opinion and digression, rather than focusing on practical information. It was first published in 1965; the extract below is from the third edition of 1967.*

Companion Guide to Venice (1967)
Hugh Honour

But the Piazza [San Marco] is beautiful at all times of day or night and all seasons of the year. It is one of the few delicate works of architecture that can absorb a bustling vulgar crowd without loss of dignity; one of the only great city squares which retains a feeling of animation when there are few people in it. I have never seen it quite empty, I must confess, for even in the early hours of a winter's morning the arcades shelter a few whispering, purposeful, loiterers. Sunshine makes the whole place glisten with gaiety, but sun is not as essential here as in most southern cities. A gauze curtain of mist gives greater grandeur to the buildings, especially if it enfolds the top of the campanile. A blanket of snow, blotting out the strange lines on the floor and exaggerating every projection on the buildings, lends a bizarre enchantment. The Piazza looks beautiful even in rain or when floods convert the centre into a huge reflecting mirror. If there is a best time to see the Piazza San Marco it is immediately after your first arrival in Venice, whatever the hour and whatever the season.

Whether you sit outside Quadri's or Florian's—where Wagner sat complaining that no one applauded his music or where Proust corrected his translation of Ruskin—it is more than probable that the people at the next table will not be Venetian. That is not to suggest that Venetians spurn these excellent cafés; but in all the more expensive resorts they are outnumbered by foreigners. For Venice has long been and still remains an international holiday city, and this is one of its many peculiarities. The traveller with historical imagination in Paris is for ever meeting the ghosts of great Frenchmen—if not Parisians—writers, generals, kings, revolutionaries: in Florence he encounters Boccaccio, Dante, Macchiavelli and the Medici. But in Venice foreigners have always formed such an important part of the scene that he jostles the shades of far more visitors than of Doges and Venetian men of letters. You walk into the Piazzetta and find Ruskin busy with his water-colours, sketching the capitals of the arcade. Or you may find Nietzsche contemplating the pigeons which form the subject of one of his most beautiful poems. At the top of the campanile stands Goethe enthusing over his first view of the sea. You turn on to the Riva degli Schiavoni and catch Proust setting off from the Danieli in a gondola for a moonlight trip with Reynaldo Hahn who sings to him—a Venetian barcarolle? Certainly not: Gounod's setting of de Musset's

> Dans Venise le rouge,
> Pas un bateau qui bouge…

From a building farther up the Riva, the bulky form of Henry James, spy-glass in hand, peers down at one. Turn the other way to the Bucintoro rowing club, in the hope of finding a spot exclusively Venetian, and there is Baron Corvo critically watching you through his pince-nez. Escape to San Lazzaro—and you find Byron helping with the translation of an Armenian grammar. And the Italians you encounter are less likely to be Venetians than visitors from Florence, or Milan or Rome—Dante surveying the Arsenal, Petrarch sitting beside the Doge in the Doges' Palace, Aretino scribbling his venomous lampoons up by the Rialto, Galileo demonstrating his telescope on the Campanile, Manzoni pondering the *Promessi Sposi* in Campo San Maurizio.

Nevertheless, the city's famous and unique charm has sometimes failed to work. Montaigne found it 'other than he imagined and not quite so wonderful.' In the eighteenth century a large number of Grand Tourists voiced their displeasure. Horace Walpole, for one, remembered only the 'pestilential air' of 'stinking ditches.' 'For God's sake let's see to arrange affairs and get out of this vile prison,' were James Adam's words on arrival in 1760. Five years later, Edward Gibbon, his mind already occupied with the *Decline and Fall*, found little that was good in the heir to a quarter of the Roman Empire. 'The spectacle of Venice afforded some hours of astonishment and some days of disgust,' he wrote. 'Old and in general ill-built houses, ruined pictures, and stinking ditches dignified with the pompous denomination of canals; a fine bridge spoilt by two rows of houses on it, and a large square decorated with the worst architecture I ever yet saw.' That same year James Boswell found that the novelty of 'so singular a city' wore off after a week and he soon 'wearied of travelling continually by water, shut up in those lugubrious gondolas.' In fact, he would have accounted his visit a waste of time had he not been able to flirt with the Signora Michieli, enjoy the favours of some whores—'strange gay ideas I had of Venetian courtesans turned my head'—and show off in the Palazzo Ducale by reciting Otway:

> Curs'd be your Senate, cursed your constitution,
> The curse of growing factions and division...

But with the cult of the picturesque, Venice returned to general favour. Even so, many voices dissented from the chorus of praise. 'I don't care a bit for it and never wish to see it again,' wrote Edward Lear of Venice in 1858; though he later changed his mind and declared 'this city of palaces, pigeons, poodles and pumpkins (I am sorry to say also of innumerable pimps—to keep up the alliteration) is a wonder and a pleasure.' 'An abhorrent, green, slippery city,' D.H. Lawrence called it—and many others have probably felt the same without saying so. Few cities in the world have aroused such extremes of adoration and dislike.

The truth is that there is something curiously melancholy and sensual in the air of Venice which irritates the full-blooded and unromantic. The whole city has the atmosphere of a deserted ballroom on the morning after a ball. Every era has supposed that 'Venice once was gay, the pleasant seat of all festivity,' but of course those days of carefree gaiety are as remote and chimerical as the golden age. Even in the last hectic carnival years of the Republic's life, when the death of a Doge was concealed for a fortnight lest it should interfere with the tourist season, the jollifications were a little hollow. You have only to look closely at the dominoed figures jigging in Francesco Guardi's pictures to feel that they are executing a dance of death: you have only to peer through the eye-holes of a *bautta* or carnival mask to see that it conceals a skull. But those who have found an echo of their own mood in this melancholy, those who have been able to savour and, like Proust and Thomas Mann, relish an atmosphere of transience and decay have fallen in love with Venice. As Henry James, with his usual percipience, wrote: 'almost every one interesting, appealing, melancholy, memorable, odd, seems at one time or another, after many days and much life, to have gravitated to Venice by a happy instinct, settling in it and treating it, cherishing it, as a sort of repository of consolations; all of which to-day, for the conscious mind, is mixed with its air and constitutes its unwritten history. The deposed, the defeated, the disenchanted, or even only the bored, have seemed to find there something that no other place could give.'

© Companion Guide to Venice, *Hugh Honour, Collins, 1967. Still in print, the most recent edition is from 2001 (Boydell & Brewer).*

JAMES HOWELL

Son of a Welsh clergyman and brother of the Bishop of Bristol, James Howell (1594–1666) was one of the first English writers to earn a living by his writing. This was not his intention: after working in a glassworks in Broad Street, London, and later as tutor to the children of various noble families, he sought promotion to public office. However, this was a time of often febrile accusation and counter-accusation in the run-up to England's civil war, which ended with the execution of King Charles I in 1649, and Howell was not sufficiently agile, lucky or well-connected to say the right thing at the right time. Nor was he any better at keeping ahead of Cromwell's 'thought-police' during the Protectorate that followed Charles I's fall. It was only in old age, following the restoration of the monarchy in 1660, that he was finally granted the post of 'Historiographer Royal'—a sort of state propagandist—with a stipend of £100 a year. Until that time he was generally short of money, spending the years 1643–51 incarcerated in the Fleet Prison. He claimed this was for his political views (he avowed a resigned, pacifist monarchism which pleased no one in those polarised times), though it was possibly for debt.

To make ends meet he had to write. The source of much of his most successful writing, in particular his Instructions for Forreigne Travel *(1642) and* Familiar Letters *(1645–55), was the three years he spent travelling in France, Spain and Italy between 1619 and 1622, in search of workers and materials for the Broad Street Glass Manufactory. He also wrote an early guide book,* Londonopolis *(1652).*

In the extracts below he writes of his professional interest—Venice's Murano glassworks—communicating with the owner of the glassworks in Broad Street, Sir Robert Mansell, whose nephew, Francis, had been Howell's tutor at Oxford. He also shrewdly observes the changes in trade routes that were already undermining Venice's pre-eminence. Howell even pens a love poem on the subject of the glass (opposite) where he acknowledges unquestioningly Murano's marketing coup in claiming that if poison were poured into a Murano glass it would immediately shatter, a handy selling point for Italy's mutually suspicious ruling families.

Upon a Cupboard of Venice Glasses.
Sent for a New Year's Gift to a Choice Lady (1621)
James Howell

Madame,
If on this New Year's gift you cast your eye,
You plainly may therein at once descry
A twofold quality; for there will appear
A brittle substance, but the Object clear.
So in the donor, Madame, you may see
These qualities inherent for to be;
His pow'r which brittle little is, Helas,
His mind sincere, and pure as any glass.
The old philosopher did wish there were
A window in his heart of chrystal clear,
Through which his friends might the more clearly see
His inward passions, and integrity.
I wish the like, for there you sure would rest
Of my clear mind, and motions of my breast.
But if it question'd be to what intent
With Venice-glasses I do you present,
I answer, that I could no gift perceive
So fit for me to give, you to receive:
For those rare Graces that in you excel,
And you that hold them, one may parallel
Unto a Venice-glass, which as 'tis clear,
And can admit no poyson to come near,
So virtue dwells in you, nor can endure
That vice should harbour in a breast so pure.

Epistolae Ho-Elianae: Familiar Letters (1645–55)
James Howell

To the Honourable Sir Robert Mansell

10th May 1621

I was, since I came hither, in Murano, a little island about the distance of Lambeth from London, where crystal glass is made, and it is a rare sight to see a whole street, where on the one side there are twenty furnaces together at work. They say here that although one should transplant a glass-furnace from Murano to Venice herself, or to any of the little assembly of islands about her, or to any other part of the earth besides, and use the same materials, the same workmen, the same fuel, the self-same ingredients every day, yet they cannot make crystal glass in that perfection, for beauty and lustre, as in Murano. Some impute it to the quality of the circumambient air that hangs over the place, which is purified and attenuated by the concurrence of so many fires that are in those furnaces night and day perpetually, for they are like the vestal fire which never goes out.

To his brother Thomas Howell, Bishop of Bristol

1st June 1621

The art of glass-making here is very highly valued; for, whosoever be of that profession are gentlemen *ipso facto*, and it is not without reason; it being a rare kind of knowledge and chemistry to transmute dust and sand (for they are the only main ingredients) to such a diaphanous pellucid dainty body as you see a crystal glass is, which hath this property above gold or silver or any other mineral, to admit no poison; as also that it never wastes or loses a whit of its first weight, though you use it never so long. When I saw so many sorts of curious glasses made here I thought upon the compliment which a gentleman put upon a lady in England, who having five or six comely daughters, said he never saw in his life such a dainty cupboard of crystal glasses; the compliment proceeds, it seems, from a saying they have here, 'That the first handsome woman that ever was made, was made of Venice glass,' which implies beauty, but brittleness withal (and Venice is not unfurnished with some of that mould, for no place abounds more with lasses and glasses). ... When I pried into the materials, and observed the furnaces and the calcinations, the transubstantiations, the liquefactions that are incident to this art, my thoughts were raised to a higher speculation: that if this small furnace-fire hath the virtue to convert such a small lump of dark dust and sand into such a precious clear body as crystal, surely that grand universal fire which shall happen at the day of judgment, may by its violent ardour vitrify and turn to one lump of crystal the whole body of the earth; nor am I the first that fell upon this conceit.

To Sir James Crofts

1st August 1621

The wealth of this republic hath been at a stand, or rather declining, since the Portugal found a road to the East Indies by the Cape of Good Hope; for this city was used to fetch all those spices and other Indian commodities from the grand Cairo down the Nile, being formerly carried to Cairo from the Red Sea upon camels' and dromedaries' backs, three-score days' journey; and so Venice used to dispense those commodities through all Christendom, which not only the Portugal, but the English and Hollander, now transport, and are masters of the trade. Yet there is no outward appearance at all of poverty, or any decay in this city, but she is still gay, flourishing, and fresh, and flowing with all kind of bravery and delight, which may be had at cheap rates. ...

I have now enough of the maiden city, and this week I am to go further into Italy; for though I have been a good while in Venice, yet I cannot say I have been hitherto upon the continent of Italy: for this city is nought else but a knot of islands in the Adriatic Sea, joined in one body by bridges, and a good way distant from the firm land. I have lighted upon very choice company, your cousin Brown and Master Web, and we all take the road of Lombardy, but we made an order amongst ourselves that our discourse be always in the language of the country, under penalty of a forfeiture, which is to be indispensably paid. ... Before I conclude I will acquaint you with a common saying that is used of this dainty city of Venice:

> 'Venetia, Venetia, chi non te vede non te pregia,
> Ma chi t'ha troppo veduto te dispreggia.'

Englished and rhymed thus (though I know you need no translation, you understand so much of Italian):

> 'Venice, Venice, none thee unseen can prize,
> Who hath seen too much will thee despise.'

Epistolae Ho-Elianae: Familiar Letters, *James Howell, Houghton, Mifflin & Co., 1907.*

WILLIAM DEAN HOWELLS

By the end of his long and active life William Dean Howells (1837–1920) was one of America's senior literary figures—the 'Dean of American Letters'—and had given Henry James (q.v) early encouragement and known Mark Twain (q.v) well. He was a proponent of 'native realism', a reaction against over-written, contrived and implausible fiction, and wrote gentle novels in which dramatic endings are eschewed as not being true to life. Probably his best known novel is The Rise of Silas Lapham (1885), one of the first in American literature to deal with the moral dilemmas of making (and, in Lapham's case, losing) a fortune in business.

In his twenties he wrote a campaign biography for Abraham Lincoln and was rewarded with the post of United States Consul to Venice. He moved there in 1861, just as the Civil War was breaking out at home and stayed for four years. At this time Venice was probably in a more depressed state than at any point in her long history: at the beginning of the century she had been invaded by Napoleon and the apparatus of her ancient republic demolished. Since 1815 she had been occupied by the Austrians, whose presence had become more visible and irksome following the crushing in 1849 of Venice's uprising and declaration of independence. Widespread poverty ensued, the Carnival was cancelled, the opera closed down, and no Venetian attended any social event at which Austrians were present. Against this gloomy background Howells, who was in later life to move as close to his hero Tolstoy's utopian socialism as his mild nature would admit, could not but feel that he was from a land 'morally and materially' superior to the one in which he found himself. He attributed the blame to the Old World in general, and to the Catholic Church in particular.

Such a feeling of superiority is never particularly attractive in travel literature, but nevertheless Howells's energy, honesty and good writing *provide a charming account of a foreigner's stay in Venice and convey a sense of his likeableness and decency.*

Having already written some poetry, in Venice Howells embarked on travel writing. It was only later that he was ready for novels. The extracts below describe his arrival in the city and a later visit to the Ghetto.

Venetian Life (1866)
William Dean Howells

All my nether-spirit, so to speak, was dulled and jaded by the long, cold railway journey from Vienna, while every surface-sense was taken and tangled in the bewildering brilliancy and novelty of Venice. For I think there can be nothing else in the world so full of glittering and exquisite surprise as that first glimpse of Venice which the traveller catches as he issues from the railway station by night, and looks upon her peerless strangeness. There is something in the blessed breath of Italy (how quickly, coming south, you know it, and how bland it is, after the harsh, transalpine air!) which prepares you for your nocturnal advent into the place; and O you! whoever you are, that journey toward this enchanted city for the first time, let me tell you how happy I count you! There lies before you for your pleasure the spectacle of such singular beauty as no picture can ever show you nor book tell you,—beauty which you shall feel perfectly but once, and regret forever.

For my own part, as the gondola slipped away from the blaze and bustle of the station down the gloom and silence of the broad canal, I forgot that I had been freezing two days and nights; that I was at that moment very cold and a little homesick. I could at first feel nothing but that beautiful silence, broken only by the star-silvered dip of the oars. Then on either hand I saw stately palaces rise gray and lofty from the dark waters, holding here and there a lamp against their faces, which brought balconies and columns and carven arches into momentary relief, and threw long streams of crimson into the canal. I could see by that uncertain glimmer how fair was all, but not how sad and old; and so, unhaunted by any pang for the decay that afterward saddened me amid the forlorn beauty of Venice, I glided on. I have no doubt it was a proper time to think all the fantastic things in the world, and I thought them; but they passed vaguely through my mind; without at all interrupting the sensations of sight and sound. Indeed, the past and present mixed there, and the moral and material were blent in the sentiment of utter novelty and surprise. The quick boat slid through old troubles of mine, and unlooked-for events gave it the impulse that carried it beyond, and safely around sharp corners of life. And all the while I knew that this was a progress through narrow and crooked canals, and past marble angles of palaces. But I did not know then that this fine confusion of sense and spirit was the first faint impression of the charm of life in Venice. Dark, funereal barges like my own had flitted by, and the gondoliers had warned each other at every turning with hoarse, lugubrious cries; the lines of balconied palaces had never ended;—here and there at their doors larger craft were moored, with dim figures of men moving uncertainly about on them. At last we had passed abruptly out of the Grand Canal into one of the smaller channels, and from comparative light into a darkness only remotely affected by some far-streaming corner lamp. But always the pallid, stately palaces; always the dark heaven with its trembling stars above, and the dark water with its trembling stars below; but now innumerable bridges, and an utter lonesomeness, and ceaseless sudden turns and windings. One could not resist a vague feeling of anxiety, in these strait and solitary passages, which was part of the strange enjoyment of the time, and which was referable to the novelty, the hush, the darkness, and the piratical appearance and unaccountable pauses of the gondoliers. Was not this Venice, and is not Venice forever associated with bravoes and unexpected dagger-thrusts? That valise of mine might represent fabulous wealth to the uncultivated imagination. Who, if I made an outcry, could understand the Facts of the Situation (as we say in the journals).

To move on was relief; to pause was regret for past transgressions mingled with good resolutions for the future. But I felt the liveliest mixture of all these emotions, when, slipping from the cover of a bridge, the gondola suddenly rested at the foot of a stairway before a closely-barred door. The gondoliers rang and rang again, while their passenger 'Divided the swift mind,' in the wonder whether a door so grimly bolted and austerely barred could possibly open into a hotel, with cheerful overcharges for candles and service. But as soon as the door opened, and he beheld the honest swindling countenance of a hotel *portier*, he felt secure against everything but imposture, and all wild absurdities of doubt and conjecture at once faded from his thought when the *portier* suffered the gondoliers to make him pay a florin too much.

So, I say, I grew early into sympathy and friendship with Venice, and, being newly from a land where everything, morally and materially, was in good repair, I rioted sentimentally on the picturesque ruin, the pleasant discomfort and hopelessness of everything about me here. It was not yet the season to behold all the delight of the lazy, out-door life of the place; but nevertheless I could not help seeing that a great part of the people, both rich and poor, seemed to have nothing to do, and that nobody seemed driven by any inward or outward impulse. When, however, I ceased (as I must in time) to be merely a spectator of this idleness, and learned that I too must assume my share of the common indolence, I found it a grievous burden. Old habits of work, old habits of hope, made my endless leisure irksome to me, and almost intolerable when I ascertained fairly and finally that, in my desire to fulfil long-cherished but, after all, merely general designs of literary study, I had forsaken wholesome struggle in the currents where I felt the motion of the age, only to drift into a lifeless eddy of the world, remote from incentive and sensation.

We had an appointment with a young Venetian lady to attend midnight mass at the San Moisè, and thither about half past eleven we went to welcome in Christmas. The church of San Moisè is in the highest style of the Renaissance art, which is, I believe, the lowest style of any other. The richly sculptured façade is divided into stories; the fluted columns are stilted upon pedestals, and their lines are broken by the bands which encircle them like broad barrelhoops. At every possible point theatrical saints and angels, only sustained from falling to the ground by iron bars let into their backs, start from the niches and cling to the sculpture. The outside of the church is in every way detestable, and the inside is consistently bad. All the side-altars have broken arches, and the high altar is built of rough blocks of marble to represent Mount Sinai, on which a melodramatic statue of Moses receives the tables of the law from God the Father, with frescoed seraphim in the background. For the same reason, I suppose, that the devout prefer a hideous Bambino and a Madonna in crinoline to the most graceful artistic conception of those sacred personages. San Moisè is the most popular church for the midnight mass in Venice, and there is no mass at all in St. Mark's where its magnificence would be so peculiarly impressive.

There never was any attempt to disturb the Hebrews by violence, except on one occasion, about the close of the Fifteenth Century, when a tumult was raised against them for child-murder. This, however, was promptly quelled by the Republic before any harm was done them; and they dwelt peacefully in their Ghetto till the lofty gates of their prison caught the sunlight of modern civilization, and crumbled beneath it.

Then many of the Jews came forth and fixed their habitations in different parts of the city, but many others clung to the spot where their temples still remain, and which was hallowed by long suffering, and soaked with the blood of innumerable generations of geese. So, although you find Jews everywhere in Venice, you never find a Christian in the Ghetto, which is held to this day by a large Hebrew population.

I do not understand why any class of Jews would still remain in the Ghetto, but it is certain, as I said, that they do remain there in great numbers. It may be that the impurity of the place and the atmosphere is conducive to purity of race; but I question if the Jews buried on the sandy slope of the Lido, and blown over by the sweet sea wind—it must needs blow many centuries to cleanse them of the Ghetto—are not rather to be envied by the inhabitants of those high dirty houses and low dirty lanes.

There was not a touch of anything wholesome, or pleasant, or attractive, to relieve the noisomeness of the Ghetto to its visitors; and they applauded, with a common voice, the neatness which had prompted Andrea the gondolier to roll up the carpet from the floor of his gondola, and not to spread it again within the limits of that quarter.

In the good old times when pestilence avenged the poor and oppressed upon their oppressors, what grim and dismal plagues may not have stalked by night and noonday out of those hideous streets, and passed the marble bounds of patrician palaces, and brought to the bedsides of the rich and proud the filthy misery of the Ghetto turned to poison!

Thank God that the good old times are going and gone! One learns in these aged lands to hate and execrate the past.

Venetian Life, *William Dean Howells, Longmans Green & Co., 1891.*

HENRY JAMES

Henry James (1843–1916) visited Venice ten times in all between 1869 (when he was only 26) and 1907 (when he was 64), sometimes staying for a period of over a month. He was fascinated by the city, appreciating its subtle appeal far more—by his own admission—than either Florence or Rome. Other writers, such as Ruskin, have written at greater length about the city, but few understood and evoked its peculiar 19th-century nature better than James: he was

Detail from a portrait by John Singer Sargent (1913).

intensely sympathetic to its powerful mixture of decay, introversion, extravagant beauty and pathos. His best-known novel, Portrait of a Lady, was written in Venice (1881), and two of his most accomplished works, The Aspern Papers (1888; see below) and The Wings of the Dove (1902; see below), are set against the backdrop of the city. In his refined and artful preface to the Portrait, James recounts how he took rooms high up above the Riva degli Schiavoni at no. 4161 (now the Pensione Wildner) and how the passage of Venetian life viewed from his eyrie was not only a distraction but also a source of inspiration:

'...the wondrous lagoon spread before me, and the ceaseless human chatter of Venice came in at my windows, to which I seem to myself to have been constantly driven, in the fruitless fidget of composition, as if to see whether, out in the blue channel, the ship of some right suggestion, of some better phrase, of the next happy twist of my subject, the next true touch for my canvas, mightn't come into sight'.

It is interesting that James talks of the 'next true touch for my canvas', because his own written style was to become more painterly with time, breaking down the clarity of his early writing into something far more allusive—almost impressionistic in feel—similar to the way in *which, say, Cézanne in his painting broke the clear outlines of forms into varying shapes of colour which together form a marvellous and convincing whole. The two extracts quoted below neatly reveal this process: the passage from The Aspern Papers, written in a clear and natural prose, with its delightful image of the tables of Florian's café on a summer's evening stretching 'like a promontory into the smooth lake of the Piazza', as against the dense and highly convoluted writing of The Wings of the Dove (a passage also describing the Piazza and Florian's). In this late style, James tiptoes around the point he is making, as if defining a circle by an infinitely qualifying number of tangential lines. The sentences are hard to focus on individually, but together they contribute to a rich and impressionistic whole. This is partly due to the fact that the manuscript was not written, but dictated to a secretary as James paced the study of his house in Rye in southeast England.*

The heroine of The Wings of the Dove, Milly Theale, is modelled on James's young cousin Minny Temple, who died of tuberculosis at the age of twenty-five; the 'Palazzo Leporelli' where Milly dies is based on the house of James's friends and hosts, Daniel and Ariana Curtis— Palazzo Barbaro. For The Aspern Papers James chose the house of another American friend, Constance Fletcher—Palazzo Soranzo Cappello on the Rio Manin at no. 770 (see map on p. 12). The garden where the passage below is set, now smaller than it was in James's day, is to the right of the palace. Tina, the niece of Juliana Bordereau, is based on another of James's cousins, the writer Constance Fenimore Woolson, who was to occupy an important and ultimately tragic place in James's life, falling to her death from a Venetian bedroom window (see map on p. 12) in 1894. Later writers have speculated that it was James's failure to reciprocate her affection that prompted her suicide.

The Aspern Papers (1888)
Henry James

I [the narrator who has taken rooms in Tina and her aunt Juliana's *palazzo* in the hope of wresting from them the papers, including

love letters to Juliana, of a famous, deceased poet, Jeffrey Aspern]
was seldom at home in the evening, for when I attempted to occupy myself in my apartments the lamplight brought in a swarm of
noxious insects, and it was too hot for closed windows. Accordingly I spent the late hours either on the water—the moonlights
of Venice are famous—or in the splendid square which serves as
a vast forecourt to the strange old church of Saint Mark. I sat in
front of Florian's café eating ices, listening to music, talking with
acquaintances: the traveller will remember how the immense
cluster of tables and little chairs stretches like a promontory into
the smooth lake of the Piazza. The whole place, of a summer's
evening, under the stars and with all the lamps, all the voices
and light footsteps on marble—the only sounds of the immense
arcade that encloses it—is an open-air saloon dedicated to cool-
ing drinks and to a still finer degustation, that of the splendid
impressions received during the day. When I didn't prefer to keep
mine to myself there was always a stray tourist, disencumbered of
his Baedeker, to discuss them with, or some domesticated painter
rejoicing in the return of the season of strong effects. The great
basilica, with its low domes and bristling embroideries, the mystery of its mosaic and sculpture, looked ghostly in the tempered
gloom, and the sea-breeze passed between the twin columns of
the Piazzetta, the lintels of a door no longer guarded, as gently
as if a rich curtain swayed there. I used sometimes on these occasions to think of the Misses Bordereau and of the pity of their
being shut up in apartments which in the Venetian July even
Venetian vastness couldn't relieve of some stuffiness. Their life
seemed miles away from the life of the Piazza, and no doubt it
was really too late to make the austere Juliana change her habits.
But poor Miss Tina would have enjoyed one of Florian's ices, I
was sure; sometimes I even had thoughts of carrying one home to
her. Fortunately my patience bore fruit and I was not obliged to
do anything so ridiculous.

One evening about the middle of July I came in earlier than
usual—I forget what chance had led to this—and instead of going

up to my quarters made my way into the garden. The temperature was very high; it was such a night as one would gladly have spent in the open air, and I was in no hurry to go to bed. I had floated home in my gondola, listening to the slow splash of the oar in the dark narrow canals, and now the only thought that occupied me was that it would be good to recline at one's length in the fragrant darkness on a garden-bench. The odour of the canal was doubtless at the bottom of that aspiration, and the breath of the garden, as I entered it, gave consistency to my purpose. It was delicious— just such an air as must have trembled with Romeo's vows when he stood among the thick flowers and raised his arms to his mistress's balcony. I looked at the windows of the palace to see if by chance the example of Verona—Verona being not far off—had been followed; but everything was dim, as usual, and everything was still. Juliana might on the summer nights of her youth have murmured down from open windows at Jeffrey Aspern, but Miss Tina was not a poet's mistress any more than I was a poet. This however didn't prevent my gratification from being great as I became aware on reaching the end of the garden that my younger padrona was seated in one of the bowers. At first I made out but an indistinct figure, not in the least counting on such an overture from one of my hostesses; it even occurred to me that some enamoured maid-servant had stolen in to keep a tryst with her sweetheart. I was going to turn away, not to frighten her, when the figure rose to its height and I recognised Miss Bordereau's niece. I must do myself the justice that I didn't wish to frighten her either, and much as I had longed for some such accident I should have been capable of retreating. It was as if I had laid a trap for her by coming home earlier than usual and by adding to that oddity my invasion of the garden. As she rose she spoke to me, and then I guessed that perhaps, secure in my almost inveterate absence, it was her nightly practice to take a lonely airing. There was no trap in truth, because I had had no suspicion. At first I took the words she uttered for an impatience of my arrival; but as she repeated them—I hadn't caught them clearly—I had the surprise of hearing her say: 'Oh dear, I'm so glad you've come!' She and her aunt had in common the property of unexpected speeches. She came out of the arbour almost as if to throw herself in my arms.

The Aspern Papers, *Henry James, Macmillan, 1888*.

The Wings of the Dove (1902)
Henry James

The weather, from early morning, had turned to storm, the first sea-storm of the autumn …

This manner, while they [Merton Densher who is pursuing the dying heiress Milly Theale in the hope of inheriting her fortune, and her sinister aged guide and servant Eugenio, protecting her out of his own self-interest] stood a long minute facing each other over all they didn't say, played a part as well in the sudden jar to Densher's protected state. It was a Venice all of evil that had broken out for them alike, so that they were together in their anxiety, if they really could have met on it; a Venice of cold lashing rain from a low black sky, of wicked wind raging through narrow passes, of general arrest and interruption, with the people engaged in all the water-life huddled, stranded and wageless, bored and cynical, under archways and bridges. Our young man's mute exchange with his friend contained meanwhile such a depth of reference that, had the pressure been but slightly prolonged, they might have reached a point at which they were equally weak. Each had verily something in mind that would have made a hash of mutual suspicion and in presence of which, as possibility, they were more united than disjoined. But it was to have been a moment for Densher that nothing could ease off—not even the formal propriety with which his interlocutor finally attended him to the *portone* and bowed upon his retreat. Nothing had passed about his coming back, and the air had made itself felt as a non-conductor of messages. Densher knew of course, as he took his way again, that Eugenio's invitation to return was not what he missed; yet he knew at the same time that what had happened to him was part of his punishment. Out in the square beyond the *fondamenta* that gave access to the landgate of the palace, out where the wind was higher, he fairly, with the thought of it, pulled his umbrella closer down. It couldn't be, his consciousness, unseen enough by others—the base predicament of having, by a concatenation, just to *take* such things: such things as the fact that one very acute person in the world, whom he couldn't dispose of as an interested scoundrel, enjoyed an opinion of him that there was no attacking, no disproving, no (what was worst of all) even noticing. One had come to a queer pass when a servant's opinion so mattered. Eugenio's would have mattered even if, as founded on a low vision of appearances, it had been quite wrong. It was the more disagreeable accordingly that the vision of appearances was quite right, and yet was scarcely less low.

Such as it was, at any rate, Densher shook it off with the more impatience that he was independently restless. He had to walk in spite of weather, and he took his course, through crooked ways, to the Piazza, where he should have the shelter of the galleries. Here, in the high arcade, half Venice was crowded close, while, on the Molo, at the limit of the expanse, the old columns of the Saint Theodore and of the Lion were the frame of a door wide open to the storm. It was odd for him, as he moved, that it should have made such a difference—if the difference wasn't only that the palace had for the first time failed of a welcome. There was more, but it came from that; that gave the harsh note and broke the spell. The wet and the cold were now to reckon with, and it was to Densher precisely as if he had seen the obliteration, at a stroke, of the margin on a faith in which they were all living. The margin had been his name for it—for the thing that, though it had held out, could bear no shock. The shock, in some form, had come, and he wondered about it while, threading his way among loungers as vague as himself, he dropped his eyes sightlessly on the rubbish in shops. There were stretches of the gallery paved with squares of red marble, greasy now with the salt spray; and the whole place, in its huge elegance, the grace of its conception and the beauty of its detail, was more than ever like a great drawing-room, the drawing-room of Europe, profaned and bewildered by some reverse of fortune. He brushed shoulders with brown men whose hats askew, and the loose sleeves of whose pendent jackets, made them resemble melancholy maskers. The tables and chairs that overflowed from the cafés were gathered, still with a pretence of service, into the arcade, and here and there a spectacled German, with his coat-collar up, partook publicly of food and philosophy. These were impressions for Densher too, but he had made the whole circuit thrice before he stopped short, in front of Florian's with the force of his sharpest. His eye had caught a face within the café—he had spotted an acquaintance behind the glass. The person he had paused long enough to look at twice was seated, well within range, at a small table on which a tumbler, half-emptied and evidently neglected, still remained; and though he had on his knee, as he leaned back, a copy of a French newspaper—the heading of the *Figaro* was visible—he stared straight before at the little opposite rococo wall. Densher had him for a minute in profile, had him for a time during which his identity produced, however quickly, all the effect of establishing connexions—connexions startling and direct; and then, as if it were the thing more needed, seized the look, determined by a turn of the head, that might have been a prompt result of the sense of being noticed. This wider view showed him *all* Lord Mark [a competitor for Milly's affections]—Lord Mark as encountered, several weeks before, the day of the first visit of each to Palazzo Leporelli. For it had been all Lord Mark that was going out, on that occasion, as he came in—he had felt in the hall, at the time; and he was accordingly the less at a loss to recognise in a few seconds, as renewed meeting brought it to the surface, the same potential quantity.

The Wings of the Dove, *Henry James, Charles Scribner's Sons, 1902.*

J.G. LINKS

Both J.G. Links (1904–97) and his wife Mary Lutyens (1908–99) are recognised scholars on the subject of Venice. Among other works, Links produced an abridged version of Ruskin's The Stones of Venice *(see p. 177) and was a leading authority on Canaletto, while Lutyens collected and edited Effie Ruskin's letters from Venice (see p. 174). In the guide book* Venice for Pleasure—'the best guide book to any city ever', *according to the* Times *columnist Bernard Levin—Links wears his great learning on the subject of Venice lightly, almost facetiously so, forever recommending the reader to leave the church / gallery / palazzo being described and to enjoy a coffee outside on the piazza instead.*

Venice for Pleasure (1966)
J.G. Links

Let us ascend the bridge and stop soon after its highest point. It is a commanding scene, indeed. Looking down the Grand Canal, towards the Salute but on the left, next to the Palazzo Cavalli, we see a pair of palaces built by the Barbaro family—the family who paid for the façade of S. Maria Zobenigo which so disgusted Ruskin and who had it devoted entirely to the glorification of their somewhat bloodthirsty exploits. 'So they have been brought to their garrets justly,' commented Ruskin to his father after he and Effie had dined with tenants in the palace's state rooms while two old brothers, the last of the Barbaros, were living in one of the garrets on the fourth floor. In the last century it was bought by a family named Curtis who used to place its 'large, cool upper floor' at the disposal of Henry James ('£40 a year to anyone but me,' he wrote to a friend). He loved Venice ('I don't care if I never see Rome or Florence again,' he added) and he loved the Barbaro so much that he resisted the temptation of buying a little house of his own, complete with garden, higher up the Grand Canal, which was offered at an absurdly cheap price. He repaid the Curtises' hospitality by placing the climax of *The Wings of the Dove* in the Palazzo Barbaro and perhaps exorcising the memories of the Barbaro family.

… Looking up the canal, we can see only as far as the Palazzo Rezzonico on the left. A tablet records that Robert Browning died there, which is true, and every gondolier and most guide books will tell you that he owned it, which is not. In fact, it had been bought in 1887 by his unpromising son, Pen, who had just married an American heiress, to Browning's delight. Pen immediately set about restoring and redecorating the gigantic building with such success that Henry James wrote home 'what he has done here with the splendid Palazzo Rezzonico transcends description for beauty.' Two years later, Browning caught cold on a visit to Pen and died; soon afterwards the American heiress could bear neither the 'stately temple of the rococo' nor Pen any longer and left, determined to become an Anglican nun. The palace had one more private owner and then, in 1935, it was sold to the Municipality who furnished it from the many eighteenth-century possessions of the Correr Museum. Fortunately for us, the amateurs' cameras were already clicking in Venice and the Brownings posed for their friend Miss Barclay outside the palace.

There are two Gothic palaces between the Rezzonico and the Accademia, the Loredan and the Contarini dagli Scrigni, and then comes the British Consul's house. On the right there are no palaces of particular note. (I should mention here that Ca' is short for Casa, or house, and that there is no significance between its use and that of the grander Palazzo as a prefix. Some very grand palaces, such as the Ca' d'Oro, are never called Palazzo; some very modest houses seem always to enjoy the name. Most of them are called by either name, just as the speaker chooses.)

The above text is taken from the 1966 edition of © Venice for Pleasure, *J.G. Links, published by Bodley Head. Reprinted by permission of The Random House Group Ltd. Still available as* Venice for Pleasure, *J.G. Links, Pallas Athene, 8th revised edition, 2008.*

THOMAS MANN

Thomas Mann, photographed in 1900.

After the death of Thomas Mann (1875–1955), his wife Katia, recalling the holiday that they had taken together in Venice in 1911, averred that the details of his story Death in Venice, which had been first published in 1912, were taken from experience: 'In the dining-room [of the Hotel des Bains], on the very first day, we saw the Polish family, exactly the way my husband described them … and the very charming, beautiful boy of about thirteen was wearing a sailor-suit, with an open collar and very pretty lacings. He caught my husband's attention immediately.' With his measured, thoughtful and finely-wrought prose (beautifully rendered here in Helen Lowe-Porter's unsurpassed translation of 1930), Mann was an aristocrat among writers. He embellished the simple tale of an older man's infatuation with a scarcely adolescent boy, with allusions to a lofty Nietzschean dichotomy between the conflicting impulses of Apollo and Dionysus, of purity and passion, within the artistic soul—a contrast which is given even clearer emphasis in Benjamin Britten's operatic version of the story (1973). The city Mann describes is a Venice perceived in all its sublime beauty on the one hand, but insidiously invaded by a cholera epidemic on the other. Brilliantly, however—as these extracts show—Mann combines this overarching theme with amusing situations which every occasional visitor to the city will recognise, for example the helplessness of the tourist in the hands of the local operators (here, the gondolier who picks Aschenbach up on his arrival), who view the visitor as little more than a source of easy money. Nor could the moment of first rapture at the extraordinariness and beauty of the city on arrival have been better captured than in this passage. And perhaps most subtly perceived of all is the way in which the city itself almost morbidly plays on our heart-strings and makes us strangely reluctant to leave and return to *the 'real world'. The story may be artificial, but Aschenbach's agonised titubation is very real to our sympathies. The object of Aschenbach's attentions—Tadzio in the story—has been identified as the young Polish nobleman Wladyslaw Moes (1900–86). The person of Gustav Aschenbach, though to some degree also autobiographical, could well have been suggested by the recent death of Gustav Mahler, which had deeply affected Mann. This connection was made explicit by Visconti's film of 1971, based on the novella.*

Death in Venice (1912)
Thomas Mann

He saw it once more, that landing-place that takes the breath away, that amazing group of incredible structures the Republic set up to meet the awe-struck eye of the approaching seafarer: the airy splendour of the palace and Bridge of Sighs, the columns of lion and saint on the shore, the glory of the projecting flank of the fairy temple, the vista of gateway and clock. Looking, he thought that to come to Venice by the station is like entering a palace by the back door. No one should approach, save by the high seas as he was doing now, this most improbable of cities.

…Is there anyone but must repress a secret thrill, on arriving in Venice for the first time—or returning thither after long absence—and stepping into a Venetian gondola? That singular conveyance, come down unchanged from ballad times, black as nothing else on earth except a coffin—what pictures it calls up of lawless, silent adventures in the plashing night; or even more, what visions of death itself, the bier and solemn rites and last soundless voyage! And has anyone remarked that the seat in such a bark, the arm-chair lacquered in coffin-black, and dully black-upholstered, is the softest, most luxurious, most relaxing seat in the world? Aschenbach realized it when he had let himself down at the gondolier's feet, opposite his luggage, which lay neatly composed on the vessel's beak. The rowers still gestured fiercely; he heard their harsh; incoherent tones. But the strange stillness of the water-city seemed to take up their voices gently, to disembody and scatter them over the sea. It was warm here in the harbour. The lukewarm air of the sirocco breathed upon him, he leaned back among his cushions and gave himself to the yielding element, closing his eyes for very pleasure in an indolence as unaccustomed as sweet. 'The trip will be short,' he thought, and wished it might last forever. They gently swayed away from the boat with its bustle and clamour of voices.

It grew still and stiller all about. No sound but the splash of the oars, the hollow slap of the wave against the steep, black, halbert-shaped beak of the vessel, and one sound more—a muttering by fits and starts, expressed as it were by the motion of his arms, from the lips of the gondolier. He was talking to himself, between his teeth. Aschenbach glanced up and saw with surprise that the lagoon was widening, his vessel was headed for the open sea. Evidently it would not do to give himself up to sweet *far niente*; he must see his wishes carried out.

'You are to take me to the steamboat landing, you know,' he said, half turning round towards it. The muttering stopped. There was no reply.

'Take me to the steamboat landing,' he repeated, and this time turned quite round and looked up into the face of the gondolier as he stood there on his little elevated deck, high against the pale grey sky. The man had an unpleasing, even brutish face, and wore blue clothes like a sailor's, with a yellow sash; a shapeless straw hat with the braid torn at the brim perched rakishly on his head. His facial structure; as well as the curling blond moustache under the short snub nose, showed him to be of non-Italian stock. Physically rather undersized, so that one would not have expected him to be very muscular, he pulled vigorously at the oar, putting all his body-weight behind each stroke. Now and then the effort he made curled back his lips and bared his white teeth to the gums. He spoke in a decided, almost curt voice, looking out to sea over his fare's head: 'The signore is going to the Lido.'…

…Thus they rowed on, rocked by the wash of a steamer returning citywards. At the landing two municipal officials were walking up and down with their hands behind their backs and their faces turned towards the lagoon. Aschenbach was helped on shore by the old man with a boat-hook who is the permanent feature of every landing-stage in Venice; and having no small change to pay the boatman, crossed over into the hotel opposite. His wants were supplied in the lobby, but when he came back his possessions were already on a hand-car on the quay, and gondola and gondolier were gone.

'He ran away, signore,' said the old boatman. 'A bad lot, a man without a licence. He is the only gondolier without one. The others telephoned over, and he knew we were on the look-out, so he made off.'

Aschenbach shrugged.

'The signore has had a ride for nothing,' said the old man, and held out his hat. Aschenbach dropped some coins. He directed that his luggage be taken to the Hotel des Bains and followed the hand-car through the avenue, that white-blossoming avenue with taverns, booths, and pensions on either side it, which runs across the island diagonally to the beach.

[*In the Hotel des Bains*]

Round a wicker table next him was gathered a group of young folk in charge of a governess or companion—three young girls, perhaps fifteen to seventeen years old, and a long-haired boy of about fourteen. Aschenbach noticed with astonishment the lad's perfect beauty. His face recalled the noblest moment of Greek sculpture—pale, with a sweet reserve, with clustering honey-coloured ringlets, the brow and nose descending in one line, the winning mouth, the expression of pure and godlike serenity. Yet with all this chaste perfection it was of such unique personal charm that the observer thought he had never seen, either in nature or art, anything so utterly happy and consummate. What struck him further was the strange contrast the group afforded, a difference in educational method, so to speak, shown in the way the brothers and sisters were clothed and treated. The girls, the eldest of whom was practically grown up, were dressed with an almost disfiguring austerity. All three wore half-length slate-coloured frocks of cloister-like plainness, arbitrarily unbecoming in cut, with white turn-over collars as their only adornment. Every grace of outline was wilfully suppressed; their hair lay smoothly plastered to their heads, giving them a vacant expression, like a nun's. All this could only be by the mother's orders; but there was no trace of the same pedagogic severity in the case of the boy. Tenderness and softness, it was plain, conditioned his existence. No scissors had been put to the lovely hair that … curled about his brows, above his ears, longer still in the neck. He wore an English sailor suit, with quilted sleeves that narrowed round the delicate wrists of his long and slender though still childish hands. And this suit, with its breast-knot, lacings, and embroideries, lent the slight figure something 'rich and strange', a spoilt, exquisite air. The observer saw him in half profile, with one foot in its black patent leather advanced, one elbow resting on the arm of his basket-chair, the cheek nestled into the closed hand in a pose of easy grace, quite unlike the stiff subservient mien which was evidently habitual to his sisters. Was he delicate? His facial tint was ivory-white against the golden darkness of his clustering locks. Or was he simply a pampered darling, the object of a self-willed and partial love? Aschenbach inclined to think the latter. For in almost every artist nature is inborn a wanton and treacherous proneness to side with the beauty that breaks hearts, to single out aristocratic pretensions and pay them homage.

———

[*Aschenbach sets off to leave Venice. In fact, he is to return to the hotel, where he dies from the cholera epidemic he was escaping.*]
It was the well-known route: through the lagoon, past San Marco, up the Grand Canal. Aschenbach sat on the circular bench in the

bows, with his elbow on the railing, one hand shading his eyes. They passed the Public Gardens, once more, the princely charm of the Piazzetta rose up before him and then dropped behind, next came the great row of palaces, the canal curved, and the splendid marble arches of the Rialto came in sight. The traveller gazed—and his bosom was torn. The atmosphere of the city, the faintly rotten scent of swamp and sea, which had driven him to leave—in what deep, tender, almost painful draughts he breathed it in! How was it he had not known, had not thought, how much his heart was set upon it all! What this morning had been slight regret, some little doubt of his own wisdom, turned now to grief, to actual wretchedness, a mental agony so sharp that it repeatedly brought tears to his eyes, while he questioned himself how he could have foreseen it. The hardest part, the part that more than once it seemed he could not bear, was the thought that he should never more see Venice again.

From Death in Venice and Seven other Stories, *Thomas Mann, translated by H.T. Lowe-Porter, © 1930, 1931, 1936 by Alfred A. Knopf, a division of Random House, Inc. Used with permission.*

JAN MORRIS

Jan Morris (b. 1926) was the journalist who 'scooped' the story of the first ascent of Mount Everest from Camp IV at 22,000 feet for The Times newspaper in 1953. A few years later he spent six months in Venice with his family, and the book Venice (The World of Venice in the United States) *was published in 1960. It was the success of this book which enabled Morris to leave full-time journalism to concentrate on history and travel writing, which she has been doing more or less ever since (Morris changed her gender in 1972). In the foreword, Morris states, 'I am a reporter, and this is primarily a report on contemporary Venice'. The extracts below cover Venice's earliest history, its everpresent lions, and Carpaccio's paintings in the Scuola di San Giorgio.*

Venice (1960)
James Morris

The estuaries of three virile rivers first formed the Venetian lagoon, rushing down from the Alps with their sediments of sand, shale and mud, and falling into the north-western corner of the Adriatic. For many centuries, sheltered from the open sea by a bulwark of sandy reefs, it remained obscure and anonymous, on the edge of the Pax Romana. Scattered communities of fishermen and salt-gatherers lived among its marshes. Traders sometimes wandered through it. A few of the Roman sporting rich built villas, picnicked, idled or hunted duck on its islands. Some historians say the people of Padua maintained a port upon its outer reefs; others believe it was much less watery then, and that half of it was under the plough. Around its perimeter, on the mainland of Roman Veneto, celebrated cities flourished—Aquileia, Concordia, Padua, Altinum, all rich in the imperial civilization: but the lagoon itself stood aside from history, and remained shrouded in myth and malaria.

Then in the fifth and sixth centuries there fell out of the north, in successive waves, the Goths, Huns, Avars, Heruleans and Lombards who were the scavengers of empire. The hinterland was lost in fire and vengeance. Driven by barbarism, brutality and even the threat of Christian heresy, the peoples of the Veneto cities abandoned their comforts and fled into their obvious refuge—the lagoon. Sometimes, when a phase of barbaric invasion had passed, they went home again: but gradually, over the years, their exodus became an emigration. They became Venetians in fits and starts. Some were ordered into the lagoon by direct divine command, and were led by their formidable bishops, clutching vestments and chalices. Some saw guiding omens, of birds, stars or saints. Some took the tools of their trades with them, even the stones of their churches. Some were destitute—'but they would receive no man of servile condition', so the traditions assure us, 'or a murderer, or of wicked life'.

Many of these people went to the northern islands of the lagoon, fringed in reeds and soggy grass (where St. Peter himself, for example, assigned one fertile estate to the citizens of Altinum). Others went to the outer perimeter, as far as possible from the fires of Attila. Gradually, in a movement sanctified by innumerable miracles and saintly interventions, the original humble islanders were overwhelmed, rights of property were established, the first Council chambers were built, the first austere churches. Venice was founded in misfortune, by refugees driven from their old ways and forced to learn new ones. Scattered colonies of city people, nurtured in all the ease of Rome, now struggled among the dank miasmas of the fenlands (their 'malarious exhalations', as Baedeker was to call them, fussily adjusting his mosquito-net 1,400 years later). They learnt to build and sail small boats, to master the treacherous tides and shallows of the lagoon, to live on fish and rain-water. They built houses of wattles and osiers, thatched and mounted on piles.

Guided by priests and patricians of the old order, they devised new institutions based upon Roman precedents: there were governing tribunes in each settlement, slowly uniting, with bickering and bloodshed, into a single administration under the presidency of a non-hereditary Doge, elected for life—'rich and poor under equal laws', said the first of Venice's innumerable sycophants, 'and envy, that curse of all the world, hath no place there'. The lagoon people were pioneers, like settlers in the early West, or colonials on the Veldt. Crèvecoeur once wrote of 'this new man, the American': but Goethe used precisely the same phrase to describe the first of the Venetians, whose old world had died around them.

Their beginnings are distinctly blurred, and were certainly not so uniformly edifying as their early apologists would have us believe. It took many years for the lagoon to spring into life and vigour; and several centuries for these new men to stop quarrelling with each other, develop into nationhood, and build the great city of Venice proper, until they could say of themselves (as they said haughtily to the Byzantine kings): 'This Venice, which we have raised in the lagoons, is our mighty habitation, and no power of Emperor or Prince can touch us !' The early chronology of Venice is hazy and debatable, and nobody really knows what happened when, if at all.

Legend, though, is always precise, and if we are to believe the old chronicles, the foundation of Venice occurred on 25th March 421, at midday exactly. It was, according to my perpetual calendar, a Friday.

On the lions of Venice
An altogether different, gentler kind of derangement informs the sculptured lions of Venice, which stand grandly apart from all these degradations. The lion became the patron beast of Venice when St. Mark became the patron saint, and for a thousand years the lion and the Serenissima were inseparable, like China and the dragon. Pope wrote contemptuously of Venice in her degeneracy as a place where

> *...Cupids ride the lion of the deeps;*
> *Where, eased of fleets, the Adriatic main*
> *Wafts the smooth eunuch and enamoured swain.*

In earlier times the lion had more honourable roles to play. He rode rampant upon the beaks of the Venetian war-galleons, and fluttered on the banner of St. Mark. His friendship for St. Jerome automatically elevated that old scholar high in the Venetian hagiarchy. He stood guard beside thrones and palaces, frowned upon prisoners, gave authenticity to the State documents of the Republic. His expression varied according to his function. In one Croatian town, after a rebellion against Venetian rule, a very disapproving lion was erected: the usual words on his open book, *Pax Tibi, Marce*, were replaced with the inscription *Let God Arise, and Let His Enemies Be Scattered*. In Zara, which revolted seven times against Venice, and withstood thirty-two Venetian sieges, a lion was erected, so the chroniclers tell us, 'with a gruff expression, his book closed and his tail contorted like an angry snake'. In a seventeenth-century map of Greece the lion is shown striding into action against the Turk, his wings outstretched, a sword in his paw, and the Doge's hat on his head. The Venetians respected him so much that some of the patricians even used to keep live lions in their gardens. A fourteenth-century writer reported excitedly that the pair in the zoological gardens beside the Basin of St. Mark's had given birth to a couple of thriving cubs: they were fed, like the pelicans of St. James's Park, at the expense of the State.

I cannot help thinking that the old Venetians went a little queer about lions, for the profusion of stone specimens in Venice is almost unbelievable. The city crawls with lions, winged lions and ordinary lions, great lions and petty lions, lions on doorways, lions supporting windows, lions on corbels, self-satisfied lions in gardens, lions rampant, lions soporific, amiable lions, ferocious lions, rickety lions, vivacious lions, dead lions, rotting lions, lions on chimneys, on flower-pots, on garden gates, on crests, on medallions, lurking among foliage, blatant on pillars, lions on flags, lions on tombs, lions in pictures, lions at the feet of statues, lions realistic, lions symbolic, lions heraldic, lions archaic, mutilated lions, chimerical lions, semi-lions, super-lions, lions with elongated tails, feathered lions, lions with jewelled eyes, marble lions, porphyry lions, and one real lion, drawn from the life, as the artist proudly says, by the indefatigable Longhi, and hung among the rest of his *genre* pictures in the Querini-Stampalia gallery. There are Greek lions, Gothic lions, Byzantine lions, even Hittite lions. There are seventy-five lions on the Porta della Carta, the main entrance to the Doge's Palace. There is a winged lion on every iron insurance plate. There is even a sorrowing lion at the foot of the Cross itself, in a picture in the Scuola di San Marco.

The most imperial lion in Venice is the winged beast painted by Carpaccio in the Doge's Palace, with a moon-lily beside his front paw, and a tail four or five feet long. The ugliest pair of lions lie at the feet of a French Ambassador's tomb in the church of San Giobbe, and were carved, with crowns on their heads and tongues slightly protruding, by the French sculptor Perreau. The silliest lion stands in the Public Gardens, removed there from the façade of the Accademia: Minerva is riding this footling beast side-saddle, and on her helmet is perched another anatomical curiosity—an owl with knees. The eeriest lion is the so-called crab-lion, which you may find in a dark archway near the church of Sant'Aponal, and which looks less like a crab than a kind of feathered ghoul. The most unassuming stands on a pillar outside San Nicolo dei Mendicoli; he holds the book of St. Mark in his paws, but has never presumed to apply for the wings. The most forward stands on a bridge near Santa Chiara, behind the car park, where a flight of steps runs fustily down to the canal like a Dickensian staircase in the shadows of London Bridge, and this unlikeable beast glowers at you like Mrs. Grundy.

The most pathetic lion is an elderly animal that stands on the palisade of the Palazzo Franchetti, beside the Accademia bridge, bearing listlessly in his mouth a label inscribed Labore. The most undernourished is a long lion on the south façade of the Basilica, three or four of whose ribs protrude cruelly through his hide. The most glamorous is the winged lion on his column in the Piazzetta, whose eyes are made of agate, whose legs were damaged when

Napoleon removed him to Paris, and whose Holy Book was inserted neatly under his paws when he was first brought to Venice from the pagan East, converted from a savage basilisk to a saint's companion.

The most indecisive lion is the creature at the foot of the Manin statue, in the Campo Manin, whose creator was evidently uncertain whether such carnivores had hair under their wings, or feathers (as Ruskin said of another pug-like example, which has fur wings, 'in several other points the manner of his sculpture is not uninteresting'). The most senile lions are the ones on the Dogana, which are losing their teeth pitifully, and look badly in need of a pension. The most long-suffering are the porphyry lions in the Piazzetta dei Leoncini, north of the Basilica, which have been used by generations of little Venetians as substitutes for rocking horses. The frankest lions, the ones most likely to succeed, are the pair that crouch, one dauntless but in chains, the other free and awfully noble, beneath the fine equestrian statue of Victor Emmanuel on the Riva degli Schiavoni.

The most enigmatical is the gaunt bald lion, outside the gates of the Arsenal, whose rump is carved with nordic runes. The most confident is the new lion that stands outside the naval school at Sant'Elena, forbidding entry to all without special permission from the commandant. The most athletic looks sinuously past the Doge Foscari on the Porta della Carta. The most threatening crouches on the façade of the Scuola di San Marco, his paws protruding, ready to leap through the surrounding marble. The most reproachful looks down from the Clock Tower in the Piazza, more in sorrow than in anger, as though he has just seen you do something not altogether creditable beneath the arcade. The jolliest—but there, none of the lions of Venice are really very unpleasant, and comparisons are invidious.

They provide an essential element in the Venetian atmosphere, an element of cracked but affectionate obsession. It is no accident that in the very centre of Tintoretto's vast Paradise, in the Doge's Palace, the lion of St. Mark sits in unobtrusive comfort, nestling beside his master amid the surrounding frenzy, and disputing with that saintly scribe, so Mark Twain thought, the spelling of an adjective.

On the Scuola di San Giorgio degli Schiavoni

Nothing anywhere is more piquantly charming than the Scuola di San Giorgio degli Schiavoni, which Carpaccio decorated, long ago, with a small series of masterpieces. It is no bigger than your garage, and its four walls positively smile with the genius of this delightful painter, the only Venetian artist with a sense of humour. Here is St. George lunging resolutely at his dragon, which is surrounded horribly by odd segments of semi-digested maidens; and here is St. Tryphonius with a very small well-behaved basilisk; and here the monks of St. Jerome's monastery, including one old brother on crutches, run in comical terror from the mildest of all possible lions; and here, in the most beguiling of all these canvases, St. Jerome himself sits in his comfortable study, looking out of his window in search of a deathless phrase, while his famous little white terrier sits bright-eyed on its haunches beside him.

The above taken from Venice, *James Morris, Faber & Faber, 1960; still in print, most recently* Venice, *Jan Morris, Faber & Faber, 2004. Excerpts from* The World of Venice, *copyright © 1974, 1960 by Jan Morris, reprinted by permission of Houghton Mifflin Harcourt Publishing Company.*

No anthology of literature on Venice would be complete without refer-
ence to one of her greatest living chroniclers writing in English. John
Julius Norwich (b. 1929) has been writing and lecturing on Venice and
other travel and historical subjects for many years. His A History of
Venice is the standard work on the subject. In the short extract below
he describes with economy Venice's eventual fall to Napoleon in 1797.

A History of Venice (1977–81)
John Julius Norwich

Neutrality is—or can be—a perfectly respectable policy; but, as
[Venetian noble] Francesco Pesaro strove to impress upon his
fellow-countrymen, it must be backed by strength. Wars between
France and Austria had almost invariably been fought out on
Italian soil; it could not now be long before Lombardy and the
Veneto were once again a battleground. When that moment came
Venice, however peaceably inclined, must show herself ready, and
able, to fight. If she were not, what hope was there that her ter-
ritorial integrity would be preserved? In her present condition,
her very existence as an independent state was in danger.

So, in debate after debate, Pesaro argued; but he argued in
vain. Once again, the opposing arguments were thin; they could
hardly have been anything else. Armed neutrality of the kind that
he advocated would necessitate a major reorganization, even a
reconstruction, of both the army and navy. How could the
Republic possibly afford such a measure, except by a swingeing
and totally unacceptable levy on private wealth? The army of the
Revolution had already turned back the invading Prussians at
Valmy and inflicted a crushing defeat on the Austrians at
Jemappes; was Pesaro seriously suggesting that Venice should
measure herself against so formidable a fighting force? As for the
idea of a Venetian army on her western frontier, what purpose
could that possibly serve except to antagonize the French unnec-
essarily and encourage them to attack?

These arguments may well have been advanced in all sincerity; but they bore no relation to the real reason for the Republic's inertia. The fact of the matter was that Venice was utterly demoralized. It was so long since she had been obliged to make a serious military effort that she had lost the will that makes such efforts possible. Peace, the pursuit of pleasure, the love of luxury, the whole spirit of *dolce far niente* had sapped her strength. She was old and tired; she was also spoilt. Even her much-vaunted constitution, once the envy of all her neighbours, seemed to be crumbling: votes were bought and sold, the effective oligarchy was shrinking steadily, the Senate was reduced to little more than a rubber stamp. In this last decade of her existence as a state, almost every political decision she made seemed calculated to hasten her end. Did she, one wonders, have a death wish? If so, it was to be granted sooner than she knew.

A History of Venice, *John Julius Norwich, Allen Lane, Penguin Press, 1982. Copyright © John Julius Norwich, 1977, 1981, 1982. Reproduced by permission of Penguin Books Ltd. Originally published in two volumes:* Venice, the Rise to Empire, *Allen Lane, 1977; and* Venice, the Greatness and the Fall, *Allen Lane, 1981.*

PETRARCH

Francesco Petrarca (1304–74), known in English as Petrarch, was one of Europe's great scholars, famed for the beauty of his sonnets and for his revival of Classical scholarship after what he called the Dark Ages, between the fall of Rome and his own time. Petrarch was a humanist: he did not reject the Church, rather he believed that the wisdom of ancient scholars and poets such as Cicero and Virgil could offer much to support traditional Christian living. In this sense, he was instrumental in allowing Roman values to

Petrarch wearing a laurel wreath to signify his coronation as Poet Laureate in 1341.

permeate medieval society without undermining it and he has been credited as a founder of the Renaissance.

Petrarch was a Tuscan, born in Arezzo to Florentine parents. A lifetime of travel began when his father moved to serve in the papal court (then at Avignon), and Petrarch studied at both Montpellier and Bologna universities. His father hoped he would become a lawyer—and Petrarch did spend some time in the papal administration—but his enthusiasm for Latin literature was stronger, and he set out on the road as a wandering scholar. He would scour monasteries for any Classical texts he could find and soon assembled an important library.

In 1361 he moved to Venice, apparently receiving a palazzo there in return for a promise to leave his books to the city. Something went wrong—it seems he was deeply hurt when he was ridiculed by some younger Venetians for his scholarship—and he left Venice to spend his final years in relative seclusion in a village near Padua. His library remained in Padua, where it was seized and broken up on his death.

Petrarch never married, but his idealisation of Laura, a married woman he glimpsed in church, was turned to good effect in his wistful sonnets. They proved enormously popular, and became a model that was used widely for love lyrics in Renaissance Europe.

In the following extract, Petrarch writes to the rhetorician Pietro Bolognese da Muglio, describing the celebrations after the Venetian defeat of a revolt in Crete.

Letters (1364)
Petrarch

To Pietro Bolognese

10th August 1364

It would take too long for my humble and busy pen to describe in words the whole series of joyful and solemn celebrations. Accept a summary. Around the sixth hour of June fourth of this year, 1364, I happened to be standing at the window looking out at the high sea…Suddenly, one of the long ships, which they call galleys, garlanded with leafy boughs, rowed into the harbour mouth, interrupting our conversation with its unexpected appearance. We at once had the premonition that it was the bearer of some happy tidings; it was clearing the channel with sails trimmed; the nimble sailors and young men, crowned with leaves and smiling broadly, waved banners aloft from the very bow and hailed the victorious fatherland, still ignorant of the news. When the ship came closer and details became visible, we noted enemy banners hanging from the stern, and no doubt remained that the ship was a messenger of victory. We were hoping for victory, not yet in the war, but in some captured city, and so our minds were incapable of grasping the reality. But when messengers came ashore and reported to the Council, all was joyful beyond our hope and beyond belief. The enemy was conquered, killed, captured, and routed, our citizens released from bondage, the cities returned to their allegiance, once again the yoke was imposed upon Crete, our victorious arms lain down; in short, the war was ended without slaughter, and peace achieved with glory.

When all this became known, Doge Lorenzo [Celsi], truly a noble man turned with all the people to praises of God and thanksgiving. Throughout the city, but more prominently in the basilica of blessed Mark the Evangelist—than which, in my opinion, none anywhere is more beautiful—everything was done that can be done for God by man. Lavish rites and an extraordinary procession were held before and around the church where not only all the laity and clergy were on hand, but also foreign prelates whom either chance or curiosity or so much talk about the ceremony had kept in town.

After the religious ceremonies had ended in splendour, everyone turned to games and spectacles. Everything was full of joy, courtesy, harmony, and love. Magnificence and pomp held sway, but without banishing modesty and sobriety; they governed and checked it as it reigned in their city and in their festivity. The celebration continued in varied pomp throughout many festive days, and at length the entire affair concluded with two spectacles, for which I have no fitting Latin words, but I shall describe them for you. One can, I believe, be called a race, the other a contest or joust. In the former the participants each ride along a straight course; in the latter they dash helter-skelter against each other. Both games are equestrian; but the first is unarmed, except that the riders with spears and shields and silk banners fluttering in the wind reflect a certain warlike image, while the second is armed, a kind of duel. Thus in the first there is the most elegance and the least danger; in the second, however, there is as much danger as skill.

Both spectacles were held in that square which I doubt has an equal in the world, before the church's marble and gold façade. They chose for this part of the celebration twenty-four noble youths, striking in appearance and dress, and summoned Tommaso Bambasio from Ferrara … Under his direction and planning, the performance was so skillfully staged and completed that you would conclude you were not seeing men riding, but angels flying—a marvelous spectacle, so many youths dressed in purple and gold, reining in and whipping on so many fleet-footed horses, so aglitter with ornaments, that their feet barely seemed to touch the ground. And they followed their captain's orders with such precision that when one reached the goal, another sprang from the mark. By this time the doge himself with a huge retinue of nobles had taken his place before the church façade above the vestibule; from this marble dais everything was beneath his feet. It is the place where those bronze and gold horses stand, as though copied from life and stampeding from above, of ancient workmanship by a superb artist, whoever he was. To shield us from the heat and glare of the setting summer sun, the whole area was provided with varicoloured awnings. I was invited there—as I am often honoured by the doge—and sat at his right.

Down below there was no empty spot, for as the saying goes, a grain of millet could not have fallen to earth; the huge square, the church itself, the towers, roofs, porches, windows were not only filled, but packed. An incalculable and incredible crowd of people covered the face of the earth; and the many large and well-dressed families of the flourishing city, spread before our eyes, doubled the joy of the festival, so that there was nothing more delightful to the populace in so much rejoicing than the sight of itself. On the right was a wooden grandstand, like a huge plat-form, built hastily just for the occasion, where four hundred young married women sat, of outstanding beauty and attire, selected from all the flower of the top nobility; and they provided elegance at midday to the spectacles, in the morning to the daily banquets, and in the evening to the entertainment under the stars. And something else that refuses to be shrouded in silence: certain high noblemen from Britain, earls and kinsmen of their king, who had lately arrived in this country by chance, took part. An overseas journey had brought them here to celebrate their recent victory and to refresh themselves meanwhile after their seafaring labours. This was the end of many days of racing games whose only prize was honour, and the same honour so equally that it could be rightly said that every man was a winner and no one a loser.

Letters from Petrarch, *translated by Morris Bishop, Indiana University Press,* © *1966. Reprinted with permission of Indiana University Press.*

The modernist poet Ezra Pound (1885–1972) first visited Venice in 1898. He lived there when he moved to Europe from Indiana in 1908 and intermittently in the 1920s and 30s. His residence became permanent from 1962 until his death in 1972, and he is buried in Venice's cemetery on the island of San Michele. Pound is closely associated with Venice's Dorsoduro district, having stayed at different times at the Pensione Seguso on the Zattere, in rented rooms in the Campo San Vio and by the church of San Trovaso, and over the years increasingly with his partner Olga Rudge in her house in Calle Querini.

In the 1940s Pound broadcast pro-Fascist and anti-semitic programmes on Italian state radio. After the fall of Mussolini, a 13-year imprisonment for treason (1945–58) awaited him, first in Pisa then in Washington, D.C. (He later remarked to the beat poet Allen Ginsberg, 'my worst mistake was the stupid, suburban prejudice of anti-semitism, all along that spoiled everything'.)

An attractive feature of Pound's writing is that, unlike many 19th-century writers in English, he is not burdened by the hackneyed view of Venice as a repository of vice and decay; rather it was for him a place of light and sparkle, a refuge and a place of recuperation. The aim of his Cantos is not to mourn that everything is getting worse, Ruskin-like (see p. 177), but to celebrate the past as part of the continuum that makes the present.

The extracts below, from Cantos XXV and XXVI (1933), illustrate Pound's magpie-like pilfering of historical vignettes to assemble his poems. He includes the story of the tardiness of Titian ('Tyciano da Cadore') in producing a painting for the Doge's Palace—it was commissioned in 1555 and only completed in 1600 by Titian's nephew, Marco Vecellio—and a claim by the painter Carpaccio that a Jerusalem painted by him had been stolen for the Duke of Mantua's court. The 'crocodile' is a reference to the dragon of St Theodore, which stands on the top of one of the two columns in the Piazzetta between St Mark's Square and the water (the other column is topped by the lion of St Mark). The description of the 'greek' clergy in Venice in the year '38 records their arrival in 1438 from Byzantium and its territories on the way to a Great Council of the Western (Roman Catholic) and

Eastern (Orthodox) churches with a view to their reunion. The Council started in Ferrara then moved at the invitation of Cosimo de' Medici in 1439 to Florence.

A Draft of XXX Cantos (1915–24)
Ezra Pound

Canto XXV

... side toward the piazza, the worst side of the room
that no one has been willing to tackle,
and do it as cheap or much cheaper...

> (signed) Tician, 31 May 1513

It being convenient that there be an end to
the painting of Titian, fourth frame from the door on
the right of the hall of the greater council, begun
by maestro Tyciano da Cadore since its being thus
unfinished holds up the decoration of said hall on
the side that everyone sees. We
move that by authority of this Council maestro Tyciano
aforesaid be constrained to finish said canvas,
and if he have not, to lose the expectancy of the
brokerage on the Fondamenta delli Thodeschi
and moreover to restore all payments recd on account of
said canvas.   11 Aug. 1522
Ser Leonardus Emo, Sapiens Consilij:
Ser Philippus Capello, Sapiens Terrae Firmae:

In 1513 on the last day of May was conceded to
Tician of Cadore painter a succession to a brokerage
on the Fondamenta dei Thodeschi, the first to be vacant
In 1516 on the 5th of December was declared that
without further waiting a vacancy he shd enter that
which had been held by the painter Zuan Bellin on

condition that he paint the picture of the land battle
in the Hall of our Greater Council on the side toward
the piazza over the Canal Grande, the which Tician after
the demise of Zuan Bellin entered into possession of the
said Sensaria and has for about twenty years profited by
it, namely to about 100 ducats a year not including the
18 to 20 ducats taxes yearly remitted him it being
fitting that as he has not worked he should not have
the said profits WHEREFORE

                                  be it moved that the said
Tician de Cadore, pictor, be by authority of this Council
obliged and constrained to restore to our government all the
moneys that he has had from the agency during the time he
has not worked on the painting in the said
hall as is reasonable

           ayes 102, noes 38,   37 undecided
                               register of the senate
                               terra 1537, carta 136.

Canto XXVI

And
I came here in my young youth
and lay there under the crocodile
By the column, looking East on the Friday,
And I said: Tomorrow I will lie on the South side
And the day after, south west.
And at night they sang in the gondolas
And in the barche with lanthorns;
The prows rose silver on silver
           taking light in the darkness. 'Relaxetur!'
11th December 1461: that Pasti be let out
                        with a caveat
'caveat ire ad Turchum, that he stay out of
                           Constantinople

'if he hold dear our govemment's pleasure.
'The book will be retained by the council'
                    (the book being Valturio's 'Re Militari').

And that year ('38) they came here
Jan. 2. The Marquis of Ferrara
        mainly to see the greek Emperor,
To take him down the canal to his house,
And with the Emperor came the archbishops:
The Archbishop of Morea Lower
And the Archbishop of Sardis
And the Bishops of Lacedaemon and of Mitylene,
Of Rhodos, of Modon Brandos,
And the Archbishops of Athens, Corinth, and of Trebizond,
The chief secretary and the stonolifex.
And came Cosimo Medici 'almost as a Venetian to Venice'
(That would be four days later)
And on the 25th, Lord Sigismundo da Rimini
For government business
And then returned to the camp.
And in February they all packed off
To Ferrara to decide on the holy ghost
And as to the which begat the what in the Trinity.—

Gemisto and the Stonolifex,
And you would have bust your bum laughing
To see the hats and beards of those greeks.

To the Marquis of Mantova, Fran° Gonzaga
Illustrious my Lord, during the past few days
An unknown man was brought to me by some others
To see a Jerusalem I have made, and as soon as he
saw it he insisted that I sell it him, saying it

gave him the gtst content and satisfac^{tn}
Finally the deal was made and he took it away,
without paying and hasn't since then appeared.
I went to tell the people who had brought him, one
of whom is a priest with a beard that wears a
grey berettino whom I have often seen with you in
the hall of the gtr council and I asked him the
fellow's name, and it is a Messire Lorenzo, the
painter to your Lordship, from which I have easily
understood what he was up to, and on that account
I am writing you, to furnish you my name and the
Work's. In the first place illustrious m lord, I am
that painter to the Seignory, commissioned to paint the
gt hall where Yr Lordship deigns to mount
on the scaffold to see our work, the history of Ancona,
and my name is Victor Carpatio.
As to the Jerusalem I dare say there is not another
in our time as good and completely perfect, or as
large. It is 25 ft. long by 5 1/2, and I know Zuane
Zamberti has often spoken of it to yr Sublimity, I
know certainly that this painter of yours has carried
off a piece, not the whole of it. I can send you
a small sketch in aquarelle on a roll, or have it
seen by good judges and leave the price to your
Lordship.
XV. Aug 1511, Venetijs.

                    I have sent a copy of
this letter by another way to be sure you get one or the other.
        The humble svt of yr Sublimity

                    Victor Carpathio,
                        pictore.

The cover of the first edition of *Temporary Kings*, published in 1973, the penultimate book in Powell's twelve-volume series *A Dance to the Music of Time* (1951–75).

The twelve-volume A Dance to the Music of Time by Anthony Powell (1905–2000) was published over a period of 25 years. Hailed at the time as 'the most remarkable sustained feat of fictional creation in our day' (The Guardian newspaper), it was immediately popular and has sold enormously, in many languages, ever since. Organised as a literary soap opera, it follows the interlocking lives of a group of English acquaintances from school days at the time of the First World War to the early 1970s. None of the characters is truly sympathetic, except possibly the narrator himself, Nicholas Jenkins, an enigmatic and self-effacing mild snob who, after Eton and the Army, works in publishing, as did Anthony Powell. By the eleventh volume, Temporary Kings, the development of the plot has been subordinated to the development of these characters: the preposterous Widmerpool, teased at school for having the wrong sort of raincoat, is now Lord Widmerpool, a Labour peer and probably spying for the Soviet Union; his man-eating wife Pamela is being pursued by sometime Hollywood mogul and press baron Louis Glober, while she in turn is pursuing the young American academic Gwinnett, who is in Venice researching a biography of X. Trapnel, a Marxist friend of Jenkins and minor writer who has recently died in a North London pub after being ditched by the same Pamela, who threw the manuscript of his last novel into a canal. Inbred and unwholesome, the series is also strangely compelling, intricately and elegantly written, often very funny, and superb social history. Here is Nicholas Jenkins's friend and fellow author-turned-publisher Mark Members persuading Jenkins to attend a literary conference held in Venice in the early 1950s, where most of Temporary Kings is set.

Temporary Kings (1973)
Anthony Powell

'All the more reason to go, Nicholas, see what such meetings of true minds have to offer. I should not be at all surprised if you did not succumb to the drug. It's quite a potent one, as I've found to my cost. Besides, even at our age, there's a certain sense of adventure at such jamborees. You meet interesting people—if writers and suchlike can be called interesting, something you and I must often have doubted in the course of our *via dolorosa* towards literary crucifixion. At worst it makes a change, provides a virtually free holiday, or something not far removed. Come along, Nicholas, bestir yourself. Say yes. Don't be apathetic.

> Leave we the unlettered plain its herd and crop;
>> Seek we sepulture
> On a tall mountain, citied to the top,
>> Crowded with culture!

It's not sepulture, and a tall mountain, this time, but the Piazza San Marco—my patron saint, please remember—and a lot of parties, not only crowded with culture, but excellent food and drink thrown in. There's the Biennale, and the Film Festival the following week, if you feel like staying for it. Kennst du das Land, wo die Zitronen blühn? Take a chance on it. You'll live like a king once you get there.'

'One of those temporary kings in *The Golden Bough*, everything at their disposal for a year or a month or a day—then execution? Death in Venice?'

'Only ritual execution in more enlightened times—the image of a declining virility. A Mann's a man for a' that. Being the temporary king is what matters. The retribution of congress kings only takes the form, severe enough in its way, I admit, of having to return to everyday life. Even that, my dear Nicholas, you'll do with renewed energy. Like the new king, in fact.

> Here upon earth, we're kings, and none but we
> Can be such kings, nor of such subjects be.

That's what the Venice Conference will amount to. I shall put your name down.'

© Temporary Kings, *Vol. 11 in* A Dance to the Music of Time *(1951–75), Anthony Powell, William Heinemann Ltd, 1973.*

MARCEL PROUST

The French novelist Marcel Proust (1871–1922) was haunted by Venice. He probably first got to know the city through the works of the English critic John Ruskin (q.v.), for which he developed a passion in the late 1890s. His first visit was with his beloved mother in May 1900 and it obviously affected him deeply. After her death in 1905 he became financially independent and was able to begin work in earnest on his A la Recherche du Temps Perdu *(Remembrance of Things Past), the vast novel which sprawled over the memories of his life and the complex relationships in Parisian high society. It was published between 1913 and 1927. Proust drew deeply on his own memories and recast them in the form of a search for the irrecoverable past. It was inevitable that Venice would feature in the novel, and the memories of the visit with his mother are entwined with the narrator's meditations on his love for the fickle Albertine, who has died following a fall from a horse. These passages show superbly how Proust uses Venice as an atmospheric setting to explore his meditations.*

Love's Sweet Cheat Gone (1925),
Volume VI of *Remembrance of Things Past*
Marcel Proust

And as I went indoors to join my mother who had left the window, I did indeed recapture, coming from the warm air outside, that feeling of coolness that I had known long ago at Combray when I went upstairs to my room, but at Venice it was a breeze from the sea that kept the air cool, and no longer upon a little wooden staircase with narrow steps, but upon the noble surfaces of blocks of marble, splashed at every moment by a shaft of greenish sunlight, which to the valuable instruction in the art of Chardin, acquired long ago, added a lesson in that of Veronese. And since at Venice it is to works of art, to things of priceless beauty, that the task is entrusted of giving us our impressions of everyday life, we may sketch the character of this city, using the pretext that the Venice of certain painters is coldly aesthetic in its most celebrated parts, by representing only (let us make an exception of the superb studies of Maxime Dethomas) its poverty-stricken aspects, in the quarters where everything that creates its splendour is concealed, and to make Venice more intimate and more genuine give it a resemblance to Aubervilliers. It has been the mistake of some very great artists, that, by a quite natural reaction from the artificial Venice of bad painters, they have attached themselves exclusively to the Venice which they have found more realistic, to some humble *campo*, some tiny deserted *rio*. It was this Venice that I used often to explore in the afternoon, when I did not go out with my mother. The fact was that it was easier to find there women of the industrial class, matchmakers, pearl-stringers, workers in glass or lace, working women in black shawls with long fringes. My gondola followed the course of the small canals; like the mysterious hand of a Genie leading me through the maze of this oriental city, they seemed, as I advanced, to be carving a road for me through the heart of a crowded quarter which they clove asunder, barely dividing with a slender fissure, arbitrarily carved, the tall houses with their tiny Moorish windows; and, as though the magic guide had been holding a candle in his hand and were lighting the way for me, they kept casting ahead of them a ray of sunlight for which they cleared a path.

After dinner, I went out by myself, into the heart of the enchanted city where I found myself wandering in strange regions like a character in the Arabian Nights. It was very seldom that I did not, in the course of my wanderings, hit upon some strange and spacious piazza of which no guidebook, no tourist had ever told me. I had plunged into a network of little alleys, *calli* dissecting in all directions by their ramifications the quarter of Venice isolated between a canal and the lagoon, as if it had crystallised along these innumerable, slender, capillary lines. All of a sudden, at the end of one of these little streets, it seemed as though a bubble had occurred in the crystallised matter. A vast and splendid *campo* of which I could certainly never, in this network of little streets, have guessed the importance, or even found room for it, spread out before me flanked with charming palaces silvery in the moonlight. It was one of those architectural wholes towards which, in any other town, the streets converge, lead you and point the way. Here it seemed to be deliberately concealed in a labyrinth of alleys, like those palaces in oriental tales to which mysterious agents convey by night a person who, taken home again before daybreak, can never again find his way back to the magic dwelling which he ends by supposing that he visited only in a dream.

On the following day I set out in quest of my beautiful nocturnal piazza, I followed *calli* which were exactly alike one another and refused to give me any information, except such as would lead me farther astray. Sometimes a vague landmark which I seemed to recognise led me to suppose that I was about to see appear, in its seclusion, solitude and silence, the beautiful exiled piazza. At that moment, some evil genie which had assumed the form of a fresh *calle* made me turn unconsciously from my course, and I found myself suddenly brought back to the Grand Canal. And as there is no great difference between the memory of a dream and the memory of a reality, I ended by asking myself whether it was not during my sleep that there had occurred in a dark patch of Venetian crystallisation that strange interruption which offered a vast piazza flanked by romantic palaces, to the meditative eye of the moon.

Love's Sweet Cheat Gone (Albertine Disparue) *Vol. VI of* Remembrance of Things Past (A La Recherche du Temps Perdu), *Marcel Proust, translated by C.K. Scott Moncrieff, 1930.*

SAMUEL ROGERS

Samuel Rogers (1763–1855) put the great wealth that he inherited to good use, self-publishing his own poetry, entertaining generously and helping out friends in financial trouble: he rescued the playwright Sheridan from eviction from his lodgings, helped Wordsworth (q.v.) obtain the post of Distributor of Stamps that gave him the financial freedom to write, and reconciled the quarrelling Byron (q.v.) and Moore .

In 1792 Rogers had written The Pleasures of Memory, *a poem that established his reputation. Twenty years later he embarked on turning his journal of a trip in Italy into a lengthy descriptive poem,* Italy, *which appeared in various forms, generally anonymously, but was only successful when published in a single version, illustrated by J.M.W. Turner, in 1830. Serving as much as a guidebook and potted history as literature it was widely read, influencing John Ruskin (q.v.) among others. Here are some extracts from the chapters on Venice, omitting the more fanciful historical re-enactments (for example where furrow-browed doges are forced to watch their own sons being tortured because their duty requires it). Given the lagoon's shallowness and tides, Ruskin later remarked on the first line that 'whereas Rogers says "There is a glorious city in the sea" a truthful person must say "There is a glorious city in the Mud".'*

Italy, a poem (1830)
Samuel Rogers

There is a glorious City in the Sea.
The Sea is in the broad, the narrow streets,
Ebbing and flowing; and the salt sea-weed
    Clings to the marble of her palaces.
No track of men, no foot-steps to and fro,
Lead to her gates. The path lies o'er the Sea,
    Invisible; and from the land we went,
    As to a floating City—steering in,
And gliding up her streets as in a dream,

So smoothly, silently—by many a dome
Mosque-like, and many a stately portico,
The statues ranged along an azure sky;
By many a pile in more than Eastern splendour,
Of old the residence of merchant-kings;
The fronts of some, tho' Time had shattered them,
Still glowing with the richest hues of art,
As though the wealth within them had run o'er.

And whence the talisman, by which she rose,
Towering? 'Twas found there in the barren sea.
Want led to Enterprise; and, far or near,
Who met not the Venetian?—now in Cairo;
Ere yet the Cafila came, listening to hear
Its bells approaching from the Red-Sea coast;
Now on the Euxine [Black Sea], on the Sea of Azoph,
In converse with the Persian, with the Russ,
The Tartar; on his lowly deck receiving
Pearls from the gulf of Ormus, gems from Bagdad;
Eyes brighter yet, that shed the light of love,
From Georgia, from Circassia. Wandering round,
When in the rich bazar he saw, displayed,
Treasures from unknown climes, away he went,
And, travelling slowly upward, drew ere-long
From the well-head, supplying all below;
Making the Imperial City of the East,
Herself, his tributary.
If we turn
To the black forests of the Rhine, the Danube,
Where o'er the narrow glen the castle hangs,
And, like the wolf that hungered at his door,
The baron lived by rapine—there we meet,
In warlike guise, the Caravan from Venice;
When on its march, now lost and now emerging,

A glittering file, the trumpet heard, the scout
Sent and recalled—but at a city-gate
All gaiety, and looked for ere it comes;
Winning its way with all that can attract,
Cages, whence every wild cry of the desert,
Jugglers, stage-dancers. Well might Charlemain,
And his brave peers, each with his visor up,
On their long lances lean and gaze awhile,
When the Venetian to their eyes disclosed
The Wonders of the East! Well might they then
Sigh for new Conquests!
Thus did Venice rise,
Thus flourish, till the unwelcome tidings came,
That in the Tagus had arrived a fleet
From India, from the region of the Sun,
Fragrant with spices—that a way was found,
A channel opened, and the golden stream
Turned to enrich another. Then she felt
Her strength departing, and at last she fell,
Fell in an instant, blotted out and razed;
She who had stood yet longer than the longest
Of the Four Kingdoms—who, as in an Ark,
Had floated down, amid a thousand wrecks,
Uninjured, from the Old World to the New,
From the last trace of civilized life—to where
Light shone again, and with unclouded splendour.

*The 'four steeds' below are the horses of St Mark's, formerly on the
façade of St Mark's basilica, now in the Museo di San Marco. The
pageant Rogers describes with knights from 'merry England' is that
described by Petrarch in 1364;* see p. 144.

… the four steeds divine,
That strike the ground, resounding with their feet,

And from their nostrils snort ethereal flame
Over that very portal—in the place
Where in an after-time Petrarch was seen
Sitting beside the Doge, on his right hand,
Amid the ladies of the Court of Venice,
Their beauty shaded from the setting sun
By many-coloured hangings; while, beneath,
Knights of all nations, some from merry England,
Their lances in the rest, charged for the prize.

On St Mark's Square

The sea, that emblem of uncertainty,
Changed not so fast for many and many an age,
As this small spot. To-day 'twas full of maskers;
And lo, the madness of the Carnival,
The monk, the nun, the holy legate masked!
To-morrow came the scaffold and the heads-man;
And he died there by torch-light, bound and gagged,
Whose name and crime they knew not.

On the prisons of Venice

That deep descent (thou canst not yet discern
Aught as it is) leads to the dripping vaults
Under the flood, where light and warmth came never!
Leads to a covered Bridge, the Bridge of Sighs;
And to that fatal closet at the foot,
Lurking for prey, which, when a victim entered,
Grew less and less, contracting to a span;
An iron-door, urged onward by a screw,
Forcing out life.—But let us to the roof,
And, when thou hast surveyed the sea, the land,

Visit the narrow cells that cluster there,
As in a place of tombs. They had their tenants,
And each supplied with sufferings of his own.
There burning suns beat unrelentingly,
Turning all things to dust, and scorching up
The brain, till Reason fled, and the wild yell
And wilder laugh, burst out on every side,
Answering each other as in mockery!

Italy *includes a loose translation of a well-known Venetian song, writ-ten by Antonio Lamberti in the 18th century:*

XIV The Gondola

Night came, and we embarked; but instantly,
Tho' she had stept on board so light of foot,
Laughing she knew not why as sure of pleasure,
She fell asleep, she slept upon my arm.
From time to time I waked her; but the boat
Rocked her to sleep again.
The moon was up,
But broken by a cloud. The wind was hushed,
And the sea mirror-like. A single zephyr
Played with her tresses, and drew more and more
Her veil across her bosom.
Long I lay
Contemplating that face so beautiful,
That rosy mouth, that cheek dimpled with smiles,
That neck but half-concealed, whiter than snow.
'Twas the sweet slumber of her early age.
I looked and looked, and felt a flush of joy
I would express but cannot.
Oft I wished
Gently—by stealth—to drop asleep myself,
And to incline yet lower that sleep might come;

Oft closed my eyes as in forgetfulness.
'Twas all in vain. Love would not let me rest.
But how delightful when at length she waked!
When, her light hair adjusting, and her veil
So rudely scattered, she resumed her place
Beside me; and, as gaily as before,
Sitting unconsciously nearer and nearer,
Poured out her innocent mind!
So, nor long since,
Sung a Venetian: and his lay of love,
Dangerous and sweet, charmed Venice. As for me
(Less fortunate, if Love be Happiness)
No curtain drawn, no pulse beating alarm,
I went alone under the silent moon;
thy place, St. Mark, thy churches, palaces,
Glittering and frost-like, and, as day drew on,
Melting away, an emblem of themselves.

Italy, *Samuel Rogers, Edward Moxon, 1830.*

¹⁶⁴ JEAN-JACQUES ROUSSEAU

Jean-Jacques Rousseau (1712–78) was one of the first to articulate many of the 18th-century Enlightenment ideas now taken for granted: he thought that man, by nature a 'noble savage', had been corrupted by the artificialities of civilisation, of private property and of material improvement. In partial contradiction he also maintained that because nature is brutal, horrid and amoral, a 'social contract' (after the title of his work Du contrat sociale, principes du droit politique; *1762), in effect a set of rules of society, is needed to order matters so that our lives are not too grim. The role of the state, he felt, is not to follow the whim of the majority but to preserve and promote freedom, equality and justice. This potent cocktail of common sense and naïvety has earned Rousseau the blame and the credit for such diverse things as the French Revolution (of which he was a posthumous hero: in 1794 he was given a fine tomb in the crypt of Paris's Panthéon), various later murderous Marxist dictatorships, and improvements in children's education: he was one of the first to stress the benefits of emotional development over book-learning.*

At the age of 16 he left Geneva, Switzerland, where he was born, and for the next 16 years he lived in various places including Piedmont, Savoy, Lyon and, for 18 months during 1743–44, in Venice, as the irregularly-paid secretary to the French ambassador. His forthright views meant he was often in trouble with governments, ecclesiastics and mobs and he became increasingly paranoid: the Scottish philosopher David Hume, with whom Rousseau sought refuge at one point, wrote to a friend 'He is plainly mad, after having long been maddish'. Here Rousseau describes, with his usual disingenuous and slightly startling frankness, his life and loves while in Venice.

The Confessions of Jean-Jacques Rousseau (1782)
Jean-Jacques Rousseau

I cannot take leave of Venice without saying something of the celebrated amusements of that city, or at least of the little part of them of which I partook during my residence there. It has been seen how little in my youth I ran after the pleasures of that age, or those that are so called. My inclinations did not change at Venice, but my occupations, which moreover would have prevented this, rendered more agreeable to me the simple recreations I permitted myself. The first and most pleasing of all was the society of men of merit. M. le Blond, de St. Cyr, Carrio Altuna, and a Porlinian gentleman, whose name I am very sorry to have forgotten, and whom I never call to my recollection without emotion: he was the man of all I ever knew whose heart most resembled my own. We were connected with two or three Englishmen of great wit and information, and, like ourselves, passionately fond of music. All these gentlemen had their wives, female friends, or mistresses: the latter were most of them women of talents, at whose apartments there were balls and concerts. There was but little play [gambling]; a lively turn, talents, and the theatres rendered this amusement insipid. Play is the resource of none but men whose time hangs heavy on their hands. I had brought with me from Paris the prejudice of that city against Italian music; but I had also received from nature a sensibility and niceness of the distinction which prejudice cannot withstand. I soon contracted that passion for Italian music with which it inspires all those who are capable of feeling its excellence. In listening to barcaroles, I found I had not yet known what singing was, and I soon became so fond of the opera that, tired of babbling, eating, and playing in the boxes when I wished to listen, I frequently withdrew from the company to another part of the theatre. There, quite alone, shut up in my box, I abandoned myself, notwithstanding the length of the representation, to the pleasure of enjoying it at ease unto the conclusion. One evening at the theatre of Saint Chrysostom, I fell into a more profound sleep than I should have done in my bed. The loud and brilliant airs did not disturb my repose. But who can explain the delicious sensations given me by the soft harmony of the angelic music, by which I was charmed from sleep; what an awaking! what ravishment! What ecstasy, when at the same instant I opened my ears and eyes! My first idea was to believe I was in paradise. The ravishing air, which I still recollect and shall never forget, began with these words:

> *Conservami la bella,*
> *Che si m'accende il cor.*

I was desirous of having it; I had and kept it for a time; but it was not the same thing upon paper as in my head. The notes were the same but the thing was different. This divine composition can never be executed but in my mind, in the same manner as it was the evening on which it awoke me from sleep.

A kind of music far superior, in my opinion, to that of operas, and which in all Italy has not its equal, nor perhaps in the whole world, is that of the *scuole*. [The famous 'ospedale'—Incurabili, Mendicanti, Ospedaletto, Pietà—where, uniquely for the time, women sang church music and extremely high musical standards were maintained: Vivaldi, for example, taught at the Pietà.] The *scuole* are houses of charity, established for the education of young girls without fortune, to whom the republic afterwards gives a portion either in marriage or for the cloister. Amongst talents cultivated in these young girls, music is in the first rank. Every Sunday at the church of each of the four *scuole*, during vespers, motettos or anthems with full choruses, accompanied by a great orchestra, and composed and directed by the best masters in Italy, are sung in the galleries by girls only; not one of whom is more than twenty years of age. I have not an idea of anything so voluptuous and affecting as this music; the richness of the art, the exquisite taste of the vocal part, the excellence of the voices, the justness of the execution, everything in these delightful concerts concurs to produce an impression which certainly is not the mode, but from which I am of opinion no heart is secure. Carrio and I never failed being present at these vespers of the Mendicanti, and we were not alone. The church was always full of the lovers of the art, and even the actors of the opera came there to form their tastes after these excellent models. What vexed me was the iron grate, which suffered nothing to escape but sounds, and concealed from me the angels of which they were worthy. I talked of nothing else. One day I spoke of it at Le Blond's: 'If you are so desirous,' said he, 'to see those little girls, it will be an easy matter to satisfy your wishes. I am one of the administrators of the house, I will give you a collation with them.' I did not let him rest until he had fulfilled his promise. On entering the saloon, which contained these beauties I so much sighed to see, I felt a trembling of love which I had never before experienced. M. le Blond presented to me, one after the other, these celebrated female singers, of whom the names and voices were all with which I was acquainted. Come, Sophia,—she was horrid. Come, Cattina,—she had but one eye. Come, Bettina,—the small-pox had entirely disfigured her. Scarcely one of them was without some striking defect. Le Blond laughed at my surprise; however, two or three of them appeared tolerable; these never sung but in the choruses; I was almost in despair. During the collation we endeavoured to excite them, and they soon became enlivened; ugliness does not exclude the graces, and I found they possessed them. I said to myself, they cannot sing in this manner without intelligence and sensibility, they must have both; in fine, my manner of seeing them changed to such a degree that I left the house almost in love with each of these ugly faces. I had scarcely courage enough to return to vespers. But after having seen the girls, the danger was lessened. I still found their singing delightful; and their voices so much embellished their persons that, in spite of my eyes, I obstinately continued to think them beautiful.

Music in Italy is accompanied with so trifling an expense, that it is not worth while for such as have a taste for it to deny themselves the pleasure it affords. I hired a harpsichord, and, for half a crown, I had at my apartment four or five symphonists, with whom I practiced once a week in executing such airs, etc., as had given me most pleasure at the opera. I also had some symphonies performed from my *Muses Galantes*. Whether these pleased the performers, or the ballet-master of St. John Chrysostom wished to flatter me, he desired to have two of them; and I had afterwards the pleasure of hearing these executed by that admirable orchestra. They were danced to by a little Bettina, pretty and amiable, and kept by a Spaniard, M. Fagoaga, a friend of ours with whom we often went to spend the evening. But apropos of girls of easy virtue: it is not in Venice that a man abstains from them. Have you nothing to confess, somebody will ask me, upon this subject? Yes: I have something to say upon it, and I will proceed to this confession with the same ingenuousness with which I have made all my former ones.

I always had a disinclination to common prostitutes, but at Venice those were all I had within my reach; most of the houses being shut against me on account of my place. The daughters of M. le Blond were very amiable, but difficult of access; and I had too much respect for the father and mother ever once to have the least desire for them.

I should have had a much stronger inclination to a young lady named Mademoiselle de Cataneo, daughter to the agent from the King of Prussia, but Carrio was in love with her: there was even between them some question of marriage. He was in easy circumstances, and I had no fortune: his salary was a hundred louis (guineas) a year, and mine amounted to no more than a thousand livres (about forty pounds sterling): and, besides, my being unwilling to oppose a friend, I knew that in all places, and especially at Venice, with a purse so ill furnished as mine was, gallantry was out of the question. I had not lost the pernicious custom of deceiving my wants. Too busily employed forcibly to feel those proceeding from the climate, I lived upwards of a year in that city as chastely as I had done in Paris, and at the end of eighteen months I quitted it without having approached the sex, except twice by means of the singular opportunities of which I am going to speak.

The first was procured me by that honest gentleman, Vitali, some time after the formal apology I obliged him to make me.

The conversation at the table turned on the amusements of Venice. These gentlemen reproached me with my indifference with regard to the most delightful of them all; at the same time extolling the gracefulness and elegant manners of the women of easy virtue of Venice; and adding that they were superior to all others of the same description in any other part of the world. Dominic said I must make the acquaintance of the most amiable of them all; and he offered to take me to her apartments, assuring me I should be pleased with her. I laughed at this obliging offer: and Count Peati, a man in years and venerable, observed to me, with more candour than I should have expected from an Italian, that he thought me too prudent to suffer myself to be taken to such a place by my enemy. In fact I had no inclination to do it: but notwithstanding this, by an incoherence I cannot myself comprehend, I at length was prevailed upon to go, contrary to my inclination, the sentiment of my heart, my reason, and even my will; solely from weakness, and being ashamed to show an appearance to the lead mistrust; and besides, as the expression of the country is, *per non parer troppo coglione* (not to appear too great a blockhead).

The Padoana whom we went to visit was pretty, she was even handsome, but her beauty was not of that kind which pleased me. Dominic left me with her, I sent for Sorbetti, and asked her to sing. In about half an hour I wished to take my leave, after having put a ducat on the table, but this by a singular scruple she refused until she had deserved it, and I from as singular a folly consented to remove her doubts. I returned to the palace so fully persuaded that I should feel the consequences of this step, that the first thing I did was to send for the king's surgeon to ask him for ptisans...

My second adventure, although likewise with a common girl, was of a nature very different, as well in its origin as in its effects. I have already said that Captain Olivet gave me a dinner on board his vessel, and that I took with me the secretary of the Spanish embassy. I expected a salute of cannon. The ship's company was drawn up to receive us, but not so much as a priming was burnt, at which I was mortified, on account of Carrio, whom I perceived to be rather piqued at the neglect. A salute of cannon was given on board merchant ships to people of less consequence than we were; I besides thought I deserved some distinguished mark of respect from the captain. I could not conceal my thoughts, because this at all times was impossible to me, and although the dinner was a very good one, and Olivet did the honours of it perfectly well, I began it in an ill humour, eating but little, and speaking still less. At the first health, at least, I expected a volley;—nothing. Carrio, who read what passed within me, laughed at hearing me grumble like a child. Before dinner was half over I saw a gondola approach the vessel. 'Bless me, sir,' said the captain, 'take care of yourself, the enemy approaches.' I asked him what he meant, and he answered jocosely. The gondola made the ship's side, and I observed a gay young damsel come on board very lightly, and coquettishly dressed, and who at three steps was in the cabin, seated by my side, before I had time to perceive a cover was laid for her. She was equally charming and lively, a brunette, not more than twenty years of age. She spoke nothing but Italian, and her accent alone was sufficient to turn my head. As she ate and chattered she cast her eyes upon me; steadfastly looked at me for a moment, and then exclaimed, 'Good Virgin! Ah, my dear Bremond, what an age it is since I saw thee!' Then she threw herself into my arms, sealed her lips to mine, and pressed me almost to strangling. Her large black eyes, like those of the beauties of the East, darted fiery shafts into my heart, and although the surprise at first stupefied my senses, voluptuousness made a rapid progress within, and this to such a degree that the beautiful seducer herself was, notwithstanding the spectators, obliged to restrain my ardor, for I was intoxicated, or rather become furious. When she perceived she had made the impression she desired, she became more moderate in her caresses, but not in her vivacity, and when she thought proper to explain to us the real or false cause of all her petulance, she said I resembled

M. de Bremond, director of the customs of Tuscany, to such a degree as to be mistaken for him; that she had turned this M. de Bremond's head, and would do it again; that she had quitted him because he was a fool; that she took me in his place; that she would love me because it pleased her so to do, for which reason I must love her as long as it was agreeable to her, and when she thought proper to send me about my business, I must be patient as her dear Bremond had been. What was said was done. She took possession of me as of a man that belonged to her, gave me her gloves to keep, her fan, her cinda, and her coif, and ordered me to go here or there, to do this or that, and I instantly obeyed her. She told me to go and send away her gondola, because she chose to make use of mine, and I immediately sent it away; she bid me to move from my place, and pray Carrio to sit down in it, because she had something to say to him; and I did as she desired. They chatted a good while together, but spoke low, and I did not interrupt them. She called me, and I approached her. 'Hark thee, Zanetto,' said she to me, 'I will not be loved in the French manner; this indeed will not be well. In the first moment of lassitude, get thee gone: but stay not by the way, I caution thee.' After dinner we went to see the glass manufactory at Murano. She bought a great number of little curiosities; for which she left me to pay without the least ceremony. But she everywhere gave away little trinkets to a much greater amount than of the things we had purchased. By the indifference with which she threw away her money, I perceived she annexed to it but little value. When she insisted upon a payment, I am of opinion it was more from a motive of vanity than avarice. She was flattered by the price her admirers set upon her favours.

In the evening we conducted her to her apartments. As we conversed together, I perceived a couple of pistols upon her toilette. 'Ah! ah!' said I, taking one of them up, 'this is a patch-box of a new construction: may I ask what is its use? I know you have other arms which give more fire than those upon your table.' After a few pleasantries of the same kind, she said to us, with an ingenuousness which rendered her still more charming, 'When I am complaisant to persons whom I do not love, I make them pay for the weariness they cause me; nothing can be more just; but if I suffer their caresses, I will not bear their insults; nor miss the first who shall be wanting to me in respect.'

At taking leave of her, I made another appointment for the next day. I did not make her wait. I found her in *vestito di confidenza*, in an undress more than wanton, unknown to northern countries, and which I will not amuse myself in describing, although I recollect it perfectly well. I shall only remark that her ruffles and collar were edged with silk network ornamented with rose-colored pompons. This, in my eyes, much enlivened a beautiful complexion. I afterwards found it to be the mode at Venice, and the effect is so charming that I am surprised it has never been introduced in France. I had no idea of the transports which awaited me. I have spoken of Madam de Larnage with the transport which the remembrance of her still sometimes gives me; but how old, ugly and cold she appeared, compared with my Zulietta! Do not attempt to form to yourself an idea of the charms and graces of this enchanting girl, you will be far too short of truth. Young virgins in cloisters are not so fresh: the beauties of the seraglio are less animated: the houris of paradise less engaging. Never was so sweet an enjoyment offered to the heart and senses of a mortal. Ah! had I at least been capable of fully tasting of it for a single moment!—I had tasted of it, but without a charm. I enfeebled all its delights: I destroyed them as at will. No; Nature has not made me capable of enjoyment. She has infused into my wretched head the poison of that ineffable happiness, the desire of which she first placed in my heart...

But, at the moment in which I was ready to faint upon a bosom, which for the first time seemed to suffer the impression of the hand and lips of a man, I perceived she had a withered teton. I struck my forehead: I examined, and thought I perceived this teton was not formed like the other. I immediately began to consider how it was possible to have such a defect, and persuaded of its proceeding from some great natural vice, I was clearly convinced, that, instead of the most charming person of whom I could form to myself an idea, I had in my arms a species of a monster, the refuse of nature, of men and of love. I carried my stupidity so far as to speak to her of the discovery I had made. She, at first, took what I said jocosely; and in her frolicsome humour, did and said things which made me die of love. But perceiving an inquietude I could not conceal she at length reddened, adjusted her dress, raised herself up, and, without saying a word, went and placed herself at a window. I attempted to place myself by her side: she withdrew to a sofa, rose from it the next moment, and fanning herself as she walked about the chamber, said to me in a reserved and disdainful tone of voice, 'Zanetto, *lascia le donne, e studia la matematica.*' (Leave women, and study the mathematics)...

These are my two adventures. The eighteen months I passed at Venice furnished me with no other of the same kind, except a simple prospect at most.

The Confessions of Jean-Jacques Rousseau, *Jean-Jacques Rousseau, translated by W. Conyngham Mallory, 1782.*

EFFIE RUSKIN

Euphemia ('Effie') Gray (1828–97) was the daughter of a Scottish lawyer. Pretty, lively and intelligent, she married the cerebral art critic John Ruskin (q.v.) in April 1848 and in the following year they travelled to Venice, staying for four months. In 1851–52 they made a second, longer visit, of almost a year. One result of their time in the city was John Ruskin's meticulously-researched The Stones of Venice. *Another was the annulment of their marriage on the grounds of non-consummation. Effie took the precaution of having her virginity medically certified and went on to marry the Pre-Raphaelite painter John Everett Millais, with whom she had eight children.*

The letters Effie wrote from Venice to her mother reveal a lively interest in all around her, considerable intelligence (in the course of her visits she added Italian to the French and German she already spoke) and great skill at the now lost art of letter-writing.

Effie in Venice: Her Picture of Society and Life with John Ruskin 1849–1852
Edited by Mary Lutyens

18th January 1850
Danieli's Hotel,

My dear Mama,

…The other day Mr Blumenthal told John that a friend of his, a Monsieur Marzari, was going to give a Concert in his house and that Mr B had asked leave to bring us if we would like to go. John said it would depend upon how I was, and when the evening came I dressed and at eight o'clock our kind little friend came for us and Charlotte and I found ourselves soon in a house near the

Rialto. John begged to be excused going as he was busy, and of course I did not wish him to lose an evening when we could go quite well here with Mr Blumenthal. We did not know what kind of party it was to be but we dressed for the evening. I had on my rose coloured silk dress, velvet roses in my hair and jacket of blue velvet trimmed with black lace which I wear always in the house and is very elegant & warm. It hangs open in front and I kept it on all the time as there was not any dancing.

When we entered the first Salon, where the music was to be, it was crowded with gentlemen but not a Lady to be seen, but on lifting a silk curtain at the end we found ourselves in a pretty little drawing room with Ladies in full dress sitting all round in the stiffest manner, but good looking, well dressed people. Mr Blumenthal presented us to Madame Marzari and then brought his sister and mother to sit by us and then went out of the Ladies Sanctum. I spoke German to the mother and French to the sister & we soon got good friends. We soon afterwards moved into the music room. The Ladies sat in two long lines and the gentlemen stood behind and talked, and between the songs came inside and spoke to their acquaintance, but instead of thinking the Italians loose in their manners I never saw such good-breeding, almost amounting to severity & prudery. The singers did not mix either with the company but had a room to themselves and when they were much applauded they curtsied and retired. In short it was like a private Theatre. The performances were of the very best description, being all the principal artists from the Fenice, so that we almost knew them before hand. The Fenice is a private Theatre—that is, it is kept up by the Nobility in Venice and not by the public. M. Marzari is one of the Three Presidents. The Count Mocenigo the second. I don't know the third.

Amongst the company, which was entirely Italian, were many Italian names I do not remember. Madame Mocenigo was not there but the Count was. It was the first time I have met him and I was not at all pleased with his appearance. He has been Ambassador to several places and is very talented, very like his old mother in appearance, but extremely dark. I believe he is a very unprincipled man and certainly to look at him you never could believe he was a descendant of the Doges who lie entombed in St. Giovanni e Paolo, each Mocenigo face finer & more beautiful than the other, even in old age.

The Prince Giovanelli & his amiable and handsome son were there. The former begged to be presented to me but I was leaving at the time and as he could not have any conversation with me he said it did not signify as Mr Brown had promised to introduce us. He is an old man much respected in Venice and the richest man here. His wife is a very sensible good person and as they are allied with Austria and live here they are popular with both parties and before the Revolution were the principal people who gave Concerts, balls and entertainments to keep the two parties on as good terms as they could, & will do so again whenever things are settled. Their only child is this young man who is very well behaved. He wishes to know us too, and Mr Brown will bring him. His name is Betta, why so I don't know. Is it not a pity that just when we are getting acquainted we must leave this nice place? But to return to the party—coffee, tea, cake & ices were the refreshments and we returned home very much pleased with our evening.

Effie in Venice: Her Picture of Society and Life with John Ruskin 1849–1852, edited by Mary Lutyens, John Murray, 1965.

JOHN RUSKIN

John Ruskin (1819–1900) is best known for his writings on art and architecture. He was both consciously old-fashioned—he often affected a wordy Victorian style for his descriptions of a lost golden age—and at the same time, and less consciously, very modern—he saw architecture as a tool for social improvement and is credited with providing the intellectual basis for the foundation of Britain's Labour Party. He was published and read widely throughout the English-speaking world, and his views were enormously influential across the arts: he was an early supporter of the Pre-Raphaelite painters; later his idealisation of the life of the artisan in contrast to that of the factory worker spawned the Arts & Crafts movement; while in architecture his bombastic attacks on Renaissance (Classical) models explained the rash of mock-Gothic buildings across Britain and North America.

His writings stretch to 39 volumes, and almost all include some reference to Venice, where he stayed in 1849–50 and 1851–52 with his wife Effie (q.v.). These extracts are taken from The Stones of Venice and illustrate themes dear to Ruskin: a romanticisation of the past, combined with an abhorrence of Classical architecture, which he saw as degenerate (as opposed to the morally uplifting Gothic). It is interesting to compare his view of Renaissance architecture such as Palladio's— 'utterly devoid of all life, virtue, honourableness, or power of doing good. It is base, unnatural, unfruitful, unenjoyable, and impious'— with Goethe's earlier admiration of Palladio's excellence (see p. 91).

The Stones of Venice (1851–53)
John Ruskin

In the olden days of travelling, now to return no more, in which distance could not be vanquished without toil, but in which that toil was rewarded, partly by the power of deliberate survey of the countries through which the journey lay, and partly by the happiness of the evening hours, when, from the top of the last hill he had surmounted, the traveller beheld the quiet village where he was to rest, scattered among the meadows beside its valley stream; or, from the long-hoped-for turn in the dusty perspective of the causeway, saw, for the first time, the towers of some famed city, faint in the rays of sunset hours of peaceful and thoughtful pleasure, for which the rush of the arrival in the railway station is perhaps not always, or to all men, an equivalent, in those days, I say, when there was something more to be anticipated and remembered in the first aspect of each successive halting-place, than a new arrangement of glass roofing and iron girder, there were few moments of which the recollection was more fondly cherished by the traveller than that which ... brought him within sight of Venice, as his gondola shot into the open lagoon from the canal of Mestre. ... [A]nd when at last that boat darted forth upon the breadth of silver sea, across which the front of the Ducal [Doge's] palace, flushed with its sanguine veins, looks to the snowy dome of Our Lady of Salvation [the Salute], it was no marvel that the mind should be so deeply entranced by the visionary charm of a scene so beautiful and so strange, as to forget the darker truths of its history and its being...

And although the last few eventful years, fraught with change to the face of the whole earth, have been more fatal in their influence on Venice than the five hundred that preceded them; though the noble landscape of approach to her can now be seen no more, or seen only by a glance, as the engine slackens its rushing on the iron line; and though many of her palaces are for ever defaced, and many in desecrated ruins, there is still so much of magic in her aspect, that the hurried traveller, who must leave her before the wonder of that first aspect has been worn away, may still be led to forget the humility of her origin, and to shut his eyes to the depth of her desolation... The Venice of modern fiction and drama is a thing of yesterday, a mere efflorescence of decay, a stage dream which the first ray of daylight must dissipate into dust. No prisoner, whose name is worth remembering, or whose sorrow deserved sympathy, ever crossed that 'Bridge of Sighs,' which is the centre of the Byronic ideal of Venice; no great merchant of Venice ever saw that Rialto under which the traveller now passes with breathless interest… The remains of [the Doges'] Venice lie hidden behind the cumbrous masses which were the delight of the nation in its dotage; hidden in many a grass-grown court, and silent pathway, and lightless canal, where the slow waves have sapped their foundations for five hundred years, and must soon prevail over them for ever. It must be our task to glean and gather them forth, and restore out of them some faint image of the lost city, more gorgeous a thousandfold than that which now exists, yet not created in the daydream of the prince, nor by the ostentation of the noble, but built by iron hands and patient hearts, contending against the adversity of nature and the fury of man, so that its wonderfulness cannot be grasped by the indolence of imagination, but only after frank inquiry into the true nature of that wild and solitary scene, whose restless tides and trembling sands did indeed shelter the birth of the city, but long denied her dominion.

On the decadence of Venice after 1423
Such, then, were the general tone and progress of the Venetian mind, up to the close of the seventeenth century. First, serious, religious, and sincere; then, though serious still, comparatively deprived of conscientiousness, and apt to decline into stern and subtle policy: in the first case, the spirit of the noble grotesque not showing itself in art at all, but only in speech and action; in the second case, devoloping itself in painting, through accessories and vivacities of composition, while perfect dignity was always preserved in portraiture. A third phase rapidly developed itself.

Once more, and for the last time, let me refer the reader to the important epoch of the death of the Doge Tomaso Mocenigo in

1423, long ago indicated as the commencement of the decline of the Venetian power. That commencement is marked, not merely by the words of the dying Prince, but by a great and clearly legible sign. It is recorded, that on the accession of his successor, Foscari, to the throne, '*Si festeggio dalla città uno anno intero.*' 'The city kept festival for a whole year.' Venice had in her childhood sown, in tears, the harvest she was to reap in rejoicing. She now sowed in laughter the seeds of death.

Thenceforward, year after year, the nation drank with deeper thirst from the fountains of forbidden pleasure, and dug for springs, hitherto unknown, in the dark places of the earth. In the ingenuity of indulgence, in the varieties of vanity, Venice surpassed the cities of Christendom, as of old she surpassed them in fortitude and devotion; and as once the powers of Europe stood before her judgment-seat, to receive the decisions of her justice, so now the youth of Europe assembled in the halls of her luxury, to learn from her the arts of delight.

It is as needless, as it is painful, to trace the steps of her final ruin. That ancient curse was upon her, the curse of the Cities of the Plain, 'Pride, fulness of bread, and abundance of idleness.' By the inner burning of her own passions, as fatal as the fiery reign of Gomorrah, she was consumed from her place among the nations; and her ashes are choking the channels of the dead salt sea.

On the evils of Classical architecture

If, then, considering these things, any of my readers should determine, according to their means, to set themselves to the revival of a healthy school of architecture in England, and wish to know in few words how this may be done, the answer is clear and simple. First, let us cast out utterly whatever is connected with the Greek, Roman, or Renaissance architecture, in principle or in form. We have seen above, that the whole mass of the architecture, founded on Greek and Roman models, which we have been in the habit of building for the last three centuries, is utterly devoid of all life, virtue, honorableness, or power of doing good. It is base, unnatural, unfruitful, unenjoyable, and impious. Pagan in its origin, proud and unholy in its revival, paralyzed in its old age, yet making prey in its dotage of all the good and living things that were springing around it in their youth, as the dying and desperate king, who had long fenced himself so strongly with the towers of it, is said to have filled his failing veins with the blood of children; an architecture invented, it seems, to make plagiarists of its architects, slaves of its workmen and Sybarites of its inhabitants; an architecture in which intellect is idle, invention impossible, but in which all luxury is gratified, and all insolence fortified;—the first thing we have to do is to cast it out, and shake the dust of it from our feet for ever. Whatever has any connexion with the five orders, or with any one of the orders,—whatever is Doric, or Ionic, or Tuscan, or Corinthian, or Composite, or in any way Grecized or Romanized; whatever betrays the smallest respect for Vitruvian laws, or conformity with Palladian work,—that we are to endure no more. To cleanse ourselves of these 'cast clouts and rotten rags' is the first thing to be done in the court of our prison.

The Stones of Venice, *John Ruskin, New York: John R. Alden, 1886.*

MARIN SANUDO

Marin Sanudo (1466–1536) was a historian and diarist who exulted in being at the centre of things during the period of Venice's greatness. His father, who died when he was a boy, was a senator but the family money was lost before Sanudo could inherit it. Even so, he was able and active and was elected a member of the Great Council when he was still under-age. This placed him close to the events of the day, and his enthusiasm for his city's past caused him to penetrate into its deepest archives. He compiled his own library, with some important documents from Venetian history, but it is perhaps his diary, kept between 1496 and 1533, which has become his most important work. It was his own boast that it would provide the best account of contemporary affairs, and it has been quarried assiduously by historians ever since.

Sanudo was writing as Venice was expanding onto the terraferma, and one of his early works details his journey on official business through Venetian-controlled territory. Another describes a war between Venice and the Duke of Ferrara. One of the most vivid accounts in the diary records the traumatic moment when news of the disastrous defeat of Venice by the French at Agnadello reached the senate chamber late in the evening of 15th May 1509. Emergency meetings of the doge and senate are held while the crowds swarm into the Doge's Palace unable to believe, as Machiavelli put it, that 800 years of history had been lost in a day. Although Venice recovered, it was as a less dynamic and more self-absorbed city, and Sanudo lived to tell of the reorientation of her politics to more sober aims.

Sanudo had a major disappointment. It had been decreed that there should be an official history of Venice. Sanudo would have been an ideal choice as chronicler, but he was passed over twice (on the second occasion the position was awarded to Pietro Bembo; q.v.). He did receive honours from his city but it was not until the early 20th century, when his diary was published in full, in 58 volumes, that his enormous contribution to the history of Venice was appreciated.

The first of the extracts below comes from a short work in praise of his city, Laus urbis Venetae, written in 1493, at a time when he could justifiably claim that it 'took pride of place before all others in prudence, fortitude, magnificence, benignity and clemency … this city was

*built more by divine than human will'. The later extracts are taken
from his diary.*

Laus Urbis Venetae (1493)
Marin Sanudo

There are two ways of getting about in Venice: by foot on the dry
land, and by boat. Certain boats are made pitch black and beautiful in shape; they are rowed by Saracen negroes or other servants who know how to row them. Mostly they are rowed with
one oar, though Venetian patricians and senators and ladies are
usually rowed with two oars. In summer the cabins have a high
covering to keep off the sun, and a broad one in winter to keep
off the rain; the high ones are of satin and the low sort green or
purple. These small boats are dismantled at night because they
are so finely wrought and each one is tied up at its mooring.
There is such an infinite number of them that they cannot be
counted; no one knows the total. On the Grand Canal and in the
rii one sees such a continual movement of boats that in a way it
is a marvel. There is easily room on them for four people, comfortably seated within. The basic cost of one of these boats is 15
ducats, but ornaments are always required, either dolphins or
other things, so that it is a great expense, costing more than a
horse. The servants, if they are not slaves, have to be paid a wage,
usually one ducat with expenses, so that adding it all up, the cost
is very high. And there is no gentleman or citizen who does not
have one or two or even more boats in the family…

The women are truly very beautiful; they go about with great
pomp adorned with jewels of enormous value and cost, neck-
laces worth from 300 up to 1,000 ducats, and rings on their
fingers set with large rubies, diamonds, sapphires, emeralds and
other jewels of great value … These ladies of ours during their
maidenhood wear veils and long tresses; then they wear a black
cape. For the most part they wear silk, and formerly they wore

gold cloth, but on account of a decree passed in the Senate they now can not do so. And, if it were not for the provisions drawn up by the most serene Signoria with regard to their tastes and desires in adornment with jewels and other things, and the regulations exacted, they would be very extravagant.

Diary entry

1st August 1513

This morning in the Criminal Court of the Forty, there was sentenced to be quartered tomorrow a certain Gasparo d'Arqua, who prowled around on the pretence of having a trembling-sickness, committing acts so hideous that they make the head reel. This man, for more than a year, had found a trade which brought here many young girls and women from the country and outside the city; and when they were on the road he took them into a certain wood and worked them over, taking any goods and money they had, threatening to kill them and made off…And he had meted out this treatment to more than eighty, among them eleven young girls who were raped, and sixteen from the city. This rogue was recognised by one of the women in the street at San Fantin, and she grabbed hold of him and handed him over to the officials. He was held in the custody of the Forty and confessed everything. Now he has been sentenced to be conveyed tomorrow on a raft up the Grand Canal, in the usual manner, then to be disembarked at Santa Croce, and dragged by a horse to San Marco, there to have his head cut off and be quartered, and the quarters to be hung on the scaffold.'

Diary entry

On 26th March, a Wednesday, some three quarters of an hour before sunset, the weather being somewhat unsettled, a mighty earthquake came upon this city of Venice. It seemed as though the houses were collapsing, the chimneys swaying, the walls bursting open, the bell-towers bending, objects in high places falling, water boiling, even in the Grand Canal as though it had been put on fire. They say that, although it was high tide, when the earthquake came some canals dried up as though there had been a tremendous drought. The earthquake lasted as long as a Miserere; all felt the sheer horror of it… The bells in their towers rang by themselves in many places, especially at St. Mark's, a terrifying thing to happen. It chanced that the Senate had just assembled to deal with affairs of state, and they had scarcely entered and begun to have a letter read when they heard the noise and felt the trembling of the chamber: then everyone jumped up, the doors were flung wide, and they descended as best they could by the wooden staircase, so quickly that some were carried from top to bottom, their feet touching none of the steps, so fierce was the stampede…

Many took it as a good omen that a battlement made of marble with lilies, the heraldic emblem of France, should fall and be destroyed—for they believed this to be God's will, for the good of Italy, which is flayed by these barbarians.

Then our Patriarch, Don Antonio Contarini, came to the Collegio, saying that the earthquake is a sign of God, and that misfortunes occur on account of sins. Venice is full of these, especially of sodomy, which is recklessly practiced everywhere. The female whores have sent to him to say that they cannot make a living because no one now goes to them, so rampant is sodomy: even the old men are getting down to it… Hence all the preachers appointed to the churches were ordered to preach, with effect from tomorrow morning, and the Patriarch ordered a three-day fast with bread and water and a procession around the public squares in the evenings, singing the litanies, with one at St. Mark's in the mornings. I applaud these things as an aid to piety and good conduct; but as a remedy for earthquakes, which are a natural phenomenon, this was no good at all.

Extracts from © Venice: A Documentary History 1450–1630, *edited by David Chambers and Brian Pullan, University of Toronto Press, 2001.*

WILLIAM SHAKESPEARE

Venice and the Veneto are the background for several scenes in Shakespeare's works: indeed Italy in general accounts for over a quarter of his settings. At times Shakespeare seems to show a quite particular knowledge of Venice, and this has encouraged some to suggest that he may actually have visited the city—possibly in 1593. As so often with events in Shakespeare's life, it cannot be proven either that he did or didn't; but it is remarkable nonetheless that he has such a clear grasp of the city's layout and a knowledge, as the examples quoted here show, of the constitution of the Venetian Republic—the equity of its laws and its tolerance and acceptance of foreigners and minorities (Shylock the Jew, Othello 'the Moor'). One cannot help feeling, though, that had an eye as sharp as Shakespeare's really been to Venice, the effect on his writing would have been far richer in detail and impression.

In Shakespeare's time, Jews had been outlawed from England since the reign of Edward I, and were to remain so up until the time of Cromwell, even though a small number of 'converso' Jews had taken refuge from Spain in Elizabethan London: one notable example, a physician named Roderigo Lopez, of Portuguese Jewish descent, had been accused of plotting to poison the Queen and had been very publicly (and probably unjustly) tried and hanged in June 1594, in an eruption of anti-semitism. This is the background of Shakespeare's The Merchant of Venice, *written probably some time before 1598. Note how, in the extract below, Shakespeare subtly draws comparisons with his own England, laying emphasis on the contrasting tolerance of the Venetian Republic toward minorities as well as its unflinching adherence to the letter of the law. He stresses the cosmopolitan nature of its society, 'Since that the trade and profit of the city / Consisteth of all nations.' Furthermore, he understands the city's law both in its*

detail and its constitution, most importantly recognising that even the
'Duke' (the Doge, in other words the head of state) can only act within
the framework of the law. One would not necessarily have to have
travelled to Venice to understand these distinctions, but some informa-
tive conversations must surely have passed between the poet and the
many Venetian merchants who came through the port of London.

The Merchant of Venice (1597)
William Shakespeare

III iii   *Venice. A street.*

Enter SHYLOCK, SALARINO, ANTONIO, *and* GAOLER

SHYLOCK

> Gaoler, look to him: tell not me of mercy;
> This is the fool that lent out money gratis:
> Gaoler, look to him.

ANTONIO   Hear me yet, good Shylock.

SHYLOCK

> I'll have my bond; speak not against my bond:
> I have sworn an oath that I will have my bond.
> Thou call'dst me dog before thou hadst a cause;
> But, since I am a dog, beware my fangs:
> The duke shall grant me justice. I do wonder,
> Thou naughty gaoler, that thou art so fond
> To come abroad with him at his request.

ANTONIO   I pray thee, hear me speak.

SHYLOCK

I'll have my bond; I will not hear thee speak:
I'll have my bond; and therefore speak no more.
I'll not be made a soft and dull-eyed fool,
To shake the head, relent, and sigh, and yield
To Christian intercessors. Follow not;
I'll have no speaking: I will have my bond.

Exit.

SALARINO

It is the most impenetrable cur
That ever kept with men.

ANTONIO

       Let him alone.
I'll follow him no more with bootless prayers.
He seeks my life; his reason well I know:
I oft deliver'd from his forfeitures
Many that have at times made moan to me;
Therefore he hates me.

SALARINO

       I am sure the duke
Will never grant this forfeiture to hold.

ANTONIO

The duke cannot deny the course of law:
For the commodity that strangers have
With us in Venice, if it be denied,
Will much impeach the justice of his state;
Since that the trade and profit of the city

Consisteth of all nations. Therefore, go:
These griefs and losses have so bated me,
That I shall hardly spare a pound of flesh
To-morrow to my bloody creditor.
Well, gaoler, on. Pray God, Bassanio come
To see me pay his debt, and then I care not!

Exeunt

IV i   *Venice. A court of justice.*

SHYLOCK

What judgement shall I dread, doing no wrong?
You have among you many a purchased slave
Which, like your asses and your dogs and mules,
You use in abject and in slavish parts,
Because you bought them: shall I say to you,
Let them be free, marry them to your heirs?
Why sweat they under burthens? Let their beds
Be made as soft as yours and let their palates
Be season'd with such viands? You will answer
'The slaves are ours': so do I answer you:
The pound of flesh, which I demand of him,
Is dearly bought; 'tis mine and I will have it.
If you deny me, fie upon your law!
There is no force in the decrees of Venice.
I stand for judgement: answer; shall I have it?

[...]
PORTIA
                                        Tarry, Jew:
The law hath yet another hold on you.
It is enacted in the laws of Venice,

If it be proved against an alien
That by direct or indirect attempts
He seek the life of any citizen,
The party 'gainst the which he doth contrive
Shall seize one half his goods; the other half
Comes to the privy coffer of the state;
And the offender's life lies in the mercy
Of the Duke only, 'gainst all other voice.
In which predicament, I say, thou stand'st;
For it appears, by manifest proceeding,
That indirectly and directly too
Thou hast contrived against the very life
Of the defendant; and thou hast incurr'd
The danger formerly by me rehearsed.
Down therefore and beg mercy of the Duke.

The Merchant of Venice, *William Shakespeare, edited by W.G. Clark and W.A. Wright, Macmillan, 1866.*

MARK TWAIN

Mark Twain (the pseudonym of Samuel Langhorne Clemens; 1835–1910) is one of the greatest American novelists. He was also a typesetter, journalist, critic, Mississippi steamboat pilot, proprietor (with his brother) of a number of newspapers, and (with a cousin) a promoter of a brilliant new mechanical typesetting machine (it didn't work and lost him a fortune).

He turned his exceptionally adventurous early life—he travelled the length and breadth of the United States, working on the Mississippi, forming a Confederate militia at the outbreak of the Civil War and disbanding it two weeks later, panning for gold in Nevada, writing for newspapers in San Francisco—into source material for numerous essays and articles, but more importantly for his novels, of which The Adventures of Tom Sawyer (1876) and its sequel The Adventures of Huckleberry Finn (1884) are probably the best known. Several years before these he had persuaded one of the San Francisco newspapers he worked for, the Alta California, to pay for him to join a cruise on the SS Quaker City as it toured the Mediterranean. The result was a series of articles on the ship's progress, with satirical descriptions of his fellow passengers. On his return it was published as a compilation entitled The Innocents Abroad or the New Pilgrim's Progress (1869), and became the best-selling of all his books in his lifetime. Here is his description, brilliant in its poetic sparkle, humour and irreverence, of arriving in Venice (compare it with William Dean Howells's more earnest but also humorous description of another arrival in Venice seven years previously; see p. 114). It illustrates Twain's incipient misanthropy, which was to engulf him in later life, but which here in his early thirties is tempered by his sense of fun and sees him singing in a flotilla of gondolas—'I sang tune after tune… I never enjoyed myself better'—only two paragraphs after lamenting that the 'old Venice of song had departed forever', its gondolas mere 'inky, rusty canoes'.

The Innocents Abroad
or the new Pilgrim's Progress (1869)
Mark Twain

This Venice, which was a haughty, invincible, magnificent Republic for nearly fourteen hundred years; whose armies compelled the world's applause whenever and wherever they battled; whose navies well nigh held dominion of the seas, and whose merchant fleets whitened the remotest oceans with their sails and loaded these piers with the products of every clime, is fallen a prey to poverty, neglect and melancholy decay. Six hundred years ago, Venice was the Autocrat of Commerce; her mart was the great commercial centre, the distributing-house from whence the enormous trade of the Orient was spread abroad over the Western world. Today her piers are deserted, her warehouses are empty, her merchant fleets are vanished, her armies and her navies are but memories. Her glory is departed, and with her crumbling grandeur of wharves and palaces about her she sits among her stagnant lagoons, forlorn and beggared, forgotten of the world. She that in her palmy days commanded the commerce of a hemisphere and made the weal or woe of nations with a beck of her puissant finger, is become the humblest among the peoples of the earth,—a peddler of glass beads for women, and trifling toys and trinkets for schoolgirls and children.

The venerable Mother of the Republics is scarce a fit subject for flippant speech or the idle gossiping of tourists. It seems a sort of sacrilege to disturb the glamour of old romance that pictures her to us softly from afar off as through a tinted mist, and curtains her ruin and her desolation from our view. One ought, indeed, to turn away from her rags, her poverty and her humiliation, and think of her only as she was when she sunk the fleets of Charlemagne; when she humbled Frederick Barbarossa or waved her victorious banners above the battlements of Constantinople.

We reached Venice at eight in the evening, and entered a hearse belonging to the Grand Hotel d'Europe. At any rate, it was more like a hearse than any thing else, though to speak by the card, it was a gondola. And this was the storied gondola of Venice!—the fairy boat in which the princely cavaliers of the olden time were wont to cleave the waters of the moonlit canals and look the eloquence of love into the soft eyes of patrician beauties, while the gay gondolier in silken doublet touched his guitar and sang as only gondoliers can sing! This the famed gondola and this the gorgeous gondolier!—the one an inky, rusty old canoe with a sable hearse-body clapped on to the middle of it, and the other a mangy, barefooted guttersnipe with a portion of his raiment on exhibition which should have been sacred from public scrutiny. Presently, as he turned a corner and shot his hearse into a dismal ditch between two long rows of towering, untenanted buildings, the gay gondolier began to sing, true to the traditions of his race. I stood it a little while. Then I said:

'Now, here, Roderigo Gonzales Michael Angelo, I'm a pilgrim, and I'm a stranger, but I am not going to have my feelings lacerated by any such caterwauling as that. If that goes on, one of us has got to take water. It is enough that my cherished dreams of Venice have been blighted forever as to the romantic gondola and the gorgeous gondolier; this system of destruction shall go no farther; I will accept the hearse, under protest, and you may fly your flag of truce in peace, but here I register a dark and bloody oath that you shan't sing. Another yelp, and overboard you go.'

I began to feel that the old Venice of song and story had departed forever. But I was too hasty. In a few minutes we swept gracefully out into the Grand Canal, and under the mellow moonlight the Venice of poetry and romance stood revealed. Right from the water's edge rose long lines of stately palaces of marble; gondolas were gliding swiftly hither and thither and disappearing suddenly through unsuspected gates and alleys; ponderous stone bridges threw their shadows athwart the glittering waves. There was life and motion everywhere, and yet everywhere there was a hush, a stealthy sort of stillness, that was suggestive of secret enterprises of bravoes and of lovers; and clad half in moonbeams and half in mysterious shadows, the grim old mansions of the Republic seemed to have an expression about them of having an eye out for just such enterprises as these at that same moment. Music came floating over the waters—Venice was complete.

It was a beautiful picture—very soft and dreamy and beautiful. But what was this Venice to compare with the Venice of midnight? Nothing. There was a fete—a grand fete in honor of some saint who had been instrumental in checking the cholera three hundred years ago, and all Venice was abroad on the water. It was no common affair, for the Venetians did not know how soon they might need the saint's services again, now that the cholera was spreading every where. So in one vast space—say a third of a mile wide and two miles long—were collected two thousand gondolas, and every one of them had from two to ten, twenty and even thirty colored lanterns suspended about it, and from four to a dozen occupants. Just as far as the eye could reach, these painted lights were massed together—like a vast garden of many-coloured flowers, except that these blossoms were never still; they were ceaselessly gliding in and out, and mingling together, and seducing you into bewildering attempts to follow their mazy evolutions. Here and there a strong red, green, or blue glare from a rocket that was struggling to get away, splendidly illuminated all the boats around it. Every gondola that swam by us, with its crescents and pyramids and circles of colored lamps hung aloft, and lighting up the faces of the young and the sweet-scented and lovely below, was a picture; and the reflections of those lights, so long, so slender, so numberless, so many-coloured and so distorted and wrinkled by the waves, was a picture likewise, and one that was enchantingly beautiful. … There was music every where—choruses, string bands, brass bands, flutes, every thing. I was so surrounded, walled in, with music, magnificence and loveliness, that I became inspired with the spirit of the scene, and sang one tune myself. However, when I observed that the other gondolas had sailed away, and my gondolier was preparing to go overboard, I stopped.

The fete was magnificent. They kept it up the whole night long, and I never enjoyed myself better than I did while it lasted.

What a funny old city this Queen of the Adriatic is! Narrow streets, vast, gloomy marble palaces, black with the corroding damps of centuries, and all partly submerged; no dry land visible any where, and no sidewalks worth mentioning; if you want to go to church, to the theatre, or to the restaurant, you must call a gondola. It must be a paradise for cripples, for verily a man has no use for legs here.

For a day or two the place looked so like an overflowed Arkansas town, because of its currentless waters laving the very doorsteps of all the houses, and the cluster of boats made fast under the windows, or skimming in and out of the alleys and byways, that I could not get rid of the impression that there was nothing the matter here but a spring freshet, and that the river would fall in a few weeks and leave a dirty high water mark on the houses, and the streets full of mud and rubbish.

In the glare of day, there is little poetry about Venice, but under the charitable moon her stained palaces are white again, their battered sculptures are hidden in shadows, and the old city seems crowned once more with the grandeur that was hers five hundred years ago. It is easy, then, in fancy, to people these silent canals with plumed gallants and fair ladies—with Shylocks in gaberdine and sandals, venturing loans upon the rich argosies of Venetian commerce—with Othellos and Desdemonas, with Iagos and Roderigos—with noble fleets and victorious legions returning from the wars. In the treacherous sunlight we see Venice decayed, forlorn, poverty-stricken, and commerceless—forgotten and utterly insignificant. But in the moonlight, her fourteen centuries of greatness fling their glories about her, and once more is she the princeliest among the nations of the earth. [*Here Twain quotes from Samuel Rogers's* Italy; *see p. 158*]

> *'There is a glorious city in the sea;*
> *The sea is in the broad, the narrow streets,*

> *Ebbing and flowing; and the salt-sea weed*
> *Clings to the marble of her palaces.*
> *No track of men, no footsteps to and fro,*
> *Lead to her gates! The path lies o'er the sea,*
> *Invisible: and from the land we went,*
> *As to a floating city—steering in,*
> *And gliding up her streets, as in a dream,*
> *So smoothly, silently—by many a dome,*
> *Mosque-like, and many a stately portico,*
> *The statues ranged along an azure sky;*
> *By many a pile, in more than Eastern pride,*
> *Of old the residence of merchant kings;*
> *The fronts of some, tho' time had shatter'd them,*
> *Still glowing with the richest hues of art,*
> *As tho' the wealth within them had run o'er.'*

What would one naturally wish to see first in Venice? The Bridge of Sighs, of course—and next the Church and the Great Square of St. Mark, the Bronze Horses, and the famous Lion of St. Mark.

We intended to go to the Bridge of Sighs, but happened into the Ducal [Doge's] Palace first—a building which necessarily figures largely in Venetian poetry and tradition. In the Senate Chamber of the ancient Republic we wearied our eyes with staring at acres of historical paintings by Tintoretto and Paul Veronese, but nothing struck us forcibly except the one thing that strikes all strangers forcibly—a black square in the midst of a gallery of portraits. In one long row, around the great hall, were painted the portraits of the Doges of Venice (venerable fellows, with flowing white beards, for of the three hundred Senators eligible to the office, the oldest was usually chosen Doge,) and each had its complimentary inscription attached—till you came to the place that should have had Marino Faliero's picture in it, and that was blank and black—blank, except that it bore a terse inscription, saying that the conspirator had died for his crime. It seemed cruel to keep that pitiless inscription still staring from the walls after the unhappy wretch had been in his grave five hundred years.

At the head of the Giant's Staircase, where Marino Faliero was beheaded, and where the Doges were crowned in ancient times, two small slits in the stone wall were pointed out—two harmless, insignificant orifices that would never attract a stranger's attention—yet these were the terrible Lions' Mouths! The heads were gone (knocked off by the French during their occupation of Venice,) but these were the throats, down which went the anonymous accusation, thrust in secretly at dead of night by an enemy, that doomed many an innocent man to walk the Bridge of Sighs and descend into the dungeon which none entered and hoped to see the sun again. This was in the old days when the Patricians alone governed Venice—the common herd had no vote and no voice. There were one thousand five hundred Patricians; from these, three hundred Senators were chosen; from the Senators a Doge and a Council of Ten were selected, and by secret ballot the Ten chose from their own number a Council of Three. All these were Government spies, then, and every spy was under surveillance himself—men spoke in whispers in Venice, and no man trusted his neighbor—not always his own brother. No man knew who the Council of Three were—not even the Senate, not even the Doge; the members of that dread tribunal met at night in a chamber to themselves, masked, and robed from head to foot in scarlet cloaks, and did not even know each other, unless by voice. It was their duty to judge heinous political crimes, and from their sentence there was no appeal. A nod to the executioner was sufficient. The doomed man was marched down a hall and out at a doorway into the covered Bridge of Sighs, through it and into the dungeon and unto his death. At no time in his transit was he visible to any save his conductor. If a man had an enemy in those old days, the cleverest thing he could do was to slip a note for the Council of Three into the Lion's mouth, saying 'This man is plotting against the Government.' If the awful Three found no proof, ten to one they would drown him anyhow, because he was a deep rascal, since his plots were unsolvable. Masked judges and masked executioners, with unlimited power, and no appeal from their judgements, in that hard, cruel age, were not likely to be lenient with men they suspected yet could not convict.

On the relics of St Mark

Of course we went to see the venerable relic of the ancient glory of Venice, with its pavements worn and broken by the passing feet of a thousand years of plebeians and patricians—The Cathedral of St. Mark. It is built entirely of precious marbles, brought from the Orient—nothing in its composition is domestic. Its hoary traditions make it an object of absorbing interest to even the most careless stranger, and thus far it had interest for me; but no further. I could not go into ecstasies over its coarse mosaics, its unlovely Byzantine architecture, or its five hundred curious interior columns from as many distant quarries. Every thing was worn out—every block of stone was smooth and almost shapeless with the polishing hands and shoulders of loungers who devoutly idled here in bygone centuries and have died and gone to the dev—no, simply died, I mean.

Under the altar repose the ashes of St. Mark—and Matthew, Luke and John, too, for all I know. Venice reveres those relics above all things earthly. For fourteen hundred years St. Mark has been her patron saint. Every thing about the city seems to be named after him or so named as to refer to him in some way—so named, or some purchase rigged in some way to scrape a sort of hurrahing acquaintance with him. That seems to be the idea. To be on good terms with St. Mark, seems to be the very summit of Venetian ambition. They say St. Mark had a tame lion, and used to travel with him—and every where that St. Mark went, the lion was sure to go. It was his protector, his friend, his librarian. And so the Winged Lion of St. Mark, with the open Bible under his paw, is a favorite emblem in the grand old city. It casts its shadow from the most ancient pillar in Venice, in the Grand Square of St.

Mark, upon the throngs of free citizens below, and has so done for many a long century. The winged lion is found every where—and doubtless here, where the winged lion is, no harm can come.

St. Mark died at Alexandria, in Egypt. He was martyred, I think. However, that has nothing to do with my legend. About the founding of the city of Venice—say four hundred and fifty years after Christ—(for Venice is much younger than any other Italian city,) a priest dreamed that an angel told him that until the remains of St. Mark were brought to Venice, the city could never rise to high distinction among the nations; that the body must be captured, brought to the city, and a magnificent church built over it; and that if ever the Venetians allowed the Saint to be removed from his new resting-place, in that day Venice would perish from off the face of the earth. The priest proclaimed his dream, and forthwith Venice set about procuring the corpse of St. Mark. One expedition after another tried and failed, but the project was never abandoned during four hundred years. At last it was secured by stratagem, in the year eight hundred and something. The commander of a Venetian expedition disguised himself, stole the bones, separated them, and packed them in vessels filled with lard. The religion of Mahomet causes its devotees to abhor any-thing that is in the nature of pork, and so when the Christian was stopped by the officers at the gates of the city, they only glanced once into his precious baskets, then turned up their noses at the unholy lard, and let him go. The bones were buried in the vaults of the grand cathedral, which had been waiting long years to receive them, and thus the safety and the greatness of Venice were secured. And to this day there be those in Venice who believe that if those holy ashes were stolen away, the ancient city would van-ish like a dream, and its foundations be buried forever in the unremembering sea.

Innocents Abroad or the New Pilgrim's Progress, *Mark Twain,* *American Publishing Company, 1869.*

GIORGIO VASARI

Venetian literature is generally impersonal: the proper subject of writing was traditionally the glorification of Venice; the whole Republic and its administration, with its ceremonial but highly constrained doge, was built on the antithesis of the cult of personality. As a result, very little is known of the characters and private lives of the famous figures in Venetian history. The great art historian Giorgio Vasari (1511–74), however, was from humanist Florence. In the mid-16th century he wrote, and later updated, The Lives of the Painters, Sculptors and Architects, *brief biographies of 60 Italian artists from the 13th to the 16th centuries. In effect one of their number himself—he designed Florence's Uffizi, for example—Vasari knew many of his later subjects personally, and his biographies bring them to life. They have served as the basis of much art history ever since.*

Vasari was particularly fond of his fellow Florentine Jacopo Sansovino, who after moving to Venice was architect of much of what still can be seen around St Mark's Square. The secret of his long and successful life was, in Vasari's opinion, hard work, plenty of fruit, and a disregard for the advice of doctors. Here are extracts from his lives of Sansovino and of Titian, the latter a much less personal portrait— though Vasari does advise him to relinquish painting in old age lest he produce inferior works which will lessen his reputation. Titian was to outlive Vasari, reaching the age of 99, his reputation entirely undiminished.

Jacopo Sansovino, Sculptor and Architect of the Venetian Republic (1486–1570)
Giorgio Vasari

Sansovino was forced to fly to Venice [from Rome in 1527, following the sack of the city by the Habsburg emperor Charles V]. He intended to proceed to France to serve the king, who had sent for him. But while he was at Venice arranging his affairs, for he had lost everything, Prince Andrea Gritti, a great patron of genius, heard of his arrival and desired to see him. It happened that at the selfsame moment Cardinal Domenico Grimani had told him that Sansovino was just the man to repair the cupola of San Marco, their principal church, which from bad foundations, age and faulty construction was cracking and threatening to fall. So Andrea sent for Jacopo, received him graciously, and after a long discussion asked him to repair the tribune. Jacopo promised, and at once began the work. He supported the whole of the interior with a wooden framework to bear the vault, securing the exterior with iron bands and shoring up the walls, while he made new foundations under the piers and rendered the building safe for ever. His work amazed Venice and pleased not only Gritti but the senate, who, as the master of the procurators of San Marco died at the time, gave Jacopo the foremost post among their engineers and architects, with the house and a good provision. In that office Jacopo showed every care for the buildings, and in the management of the accounts and books, and in all the duties of his position. He became very friendly with the rulers, rendering their things grand and beautiful, making the church, city and piazza more beautiful than any previous holder of the office had done, illuminating everything by his genius, though with little or no expense to the rulers. ... By the order of the procurators, he began [in 1536] the beautiful and rich library opposite the public palace, in the Corinthian and Doric orders, with carvings, cornices, columns, capitals and half-length figures everywhere, without sparing any expense, for it is full of rich pavements, stucco scenes in the rooms and public staircases decorated with paintings ... besides having many rich ornaments which give majesty and grandeur to the principal door, all of which go to prove Sansovino's great ability. This has led to all houses and palaces in the city, which were formerly built in the same style in the same proportions, being erected with new designs and better order, following Vitruvius. This work is considered peerless by many good judges who have seen much of the world. ... But the finest, richest and strongest of Jacopo's buildings is the mint of Venice, constructed entirely of iron and stone, without a scrap of wood, as a precaution against fire. The interior is conveniently arranged, no mint in the world being so well adapted for the work, or so strong. It is entirely in rustic-work, not seen before in that city, where it excited considerable wonder. … Very wonderful and novel was his work for the Tiepoli at the Misericordia, in making new foundations of large stones under their sumptuous palace on the Grand Canal, which owing to bad foundations would have fallen in a few years, while the owners now live there in absolute safety. In spite of these numerous buildings, he never ceased to make beautiful works in marble and bronze for his own delight. Above the holy water-vessel of the friars of ca Grande [in the Frari] is an admirable marble St. John the Baptist by him.

At the bottom of the steps of the palace of San Marco he made two colossal figures, seven braccia high, of Neptune and Mars, to show the power of the republic by land and sea, and did six bronze half-reliefs for San Marco of the life of St Mark, one braccia long by one and a half high, to decorate a pulpit, which are much prized for their variety. Over the door of San Marco he did a life-size marble Virgin, considered very beautiful. The bronze door of the sacristy is also his. It is divided into two parts, containing scenes from the life of Christ excellently done in half-relief. Over the arsenal door he did a beautiful marble Virgin and Child. All these works have at once adorned the republic, displayed the genius of Sansovino and the magnificence and liberality of the rulers and also of the artists, in giving him all the sculpture and architecture executed in the city in his day. In truth, Jacopo's ability merited the recognition of his pre-eminent position in the city among artists, and nobles and common people alike admired his talent. Among other things his knowledge and judgment have practically renewed the city, where he has taught the true methods of building.

The Works of Titian of Cadore, Painter (1477–1576)
Giorgio Vasari

Titian was born at Cadore, a little village on the Piave, five miles from the foot of the Alps, in 1480, of the Vecelli family, one of the noblest there. At the age of ten he showed great intelligence, and was sent to an uncle, an honoured citizen of Venice, who perceived his bent for painting and put him with Gian Bellini, a famous painter of the time, to study design, where he soon displayed his natural intelligence and judgment, which are necessary to painting. Gian Bellini and the other painters of the country, through not having studied antiquities, employed a hard, dry and laboured style, which Titian acquired. But in 1507 arose Giorgione, who began to give his works more tone and relief, with better style, though he imitated natural things as best he could, colouring them like life, without making drawings previously, believing this to be the true method of procedure. He did not perceive that for good composition it is necessary to try several various methods on sheets, for invention is quickened by showing these things to the eye, while it is also necessary to a thorough knowledge of the nude. Besides, to have nude or draped models always before the eyes is no small tax. Thus by means of drawings it becomes easier to work out a composition, and so become skilful and judicious without the labour of making paintings as already described, not to mention that drawing fills the mind with good ideas; and one learns to retain natural objects in the head without it being necessary to have them always at hand, and to be obliged to conceal inability to draw by splendour of colouring as the Venetian painters have done for many years, for example Giorgione, Palma, Pordenone, and others who did not see Rome or perfect works.

On seeing Giorgione's style Titian abandoned that of Bellini, although he had long practised it, and imitated Giorgione so well that in a short time his works were taken for Giorgione's. As he advanced in years, skill and good judgment Titian did many frescoes, which I cannot describe in order, as they are scattered in many places. Skilled judges, however, considered that they showed promise of a great future. When he first adopted Giorgione's style, at the age of eighteen, he made the portrait of a noble of ca Barbarigo, his friend, considered very beautiful for the natural flesh-colour, the hairs which might be counted, and the points of a doublet of smooth silvered material. It was so excellent that, if Titian had not written his name on the dark background, it would have been attributed to Giorgione.

That master having done the façade of the Fondaco de' Tedeschi, Barbarigo succeeded in having some scenes on the same building facing the Merceria allotted to Titian. … Many nobles not being aware that Giorgione had been replaced, or that Titian was engaged there, met the former and congratulated him on his greater success with the façade towards the Merceria than with that on the Grand Canal. Giorgione felt so mortified at this that, until Titian had finished all the work and it was well known that he had done that section, Giorgione largely refrained from appearing in public, and thenceforward he refused to hold intercourse with Titian or be friends with him.

Having now reached the age of seventy-six, he has always been a most healthy and fortunate man, beyond any of his fellows, and has received nothing but favours from Heaven. His house at Venice has been frequented by all the princes, learned men and gallants of his time, because in addition to his genius he possesses the most courtly manners. He has had some rivals in Venice whom he has easily surpassed, and he has retained the favour of the nobles. He has gained much wealth, as his works have been well paid for, and in his latter years he would have done well to have worked only for amusement, in order not to circulate works which may damage a reputation won in his best years. When the present writer was in Venice in 1566 he visited Titian as his friend, and found him, old as he was, engaged in

painting. I was pleased to see his works and to talk with him. ...
Titian therefore having adorned Venice, Italy and other parts of
the world with noble paintings, deserves the honour of artists,
and to be imitated in many things, for his works will endure as
long as the memory of famous men.

The Lives of the Painters, Sculptors and Architects, *Giorgio Vasari, Vol.
4, translated by A.B. Hinds, Everyman's Library, J.M. Dent & Sons, 1927.*

RICHARD WAGNER

Richard Wagner (1813–83) was no stranger to living in foreign lands: for twelve years between 1849 and 1861 he lived in France, and then mostly in Switzerland, exiled from his homeland of Saxony for his 'revolutionary' views and his participation in the Dresden Uprising of 1849. This past returned to haunt him: his first visit to Venice at the age of 45 in 1858–59 ended after less than a year because the authorities in Saxony had called for his expulsion from all Austrian territory, to which Venice then belonged. Wagner was to visit Venice six times in all, as the city grew in his affection. He loved it for its quiet and tranquillity. It cocooned him and cut him off from the outside world, giving him the psychological peace and protection to absorb himself fully in his work of composition. It was not easy, though, for someone as prominent as Wagner to keep himself isolated: his lodgings in Venice were often filled with friends, composers and admirers. In the evenings, too, when he dined in St Mark's Square, he found himself in the curious predicament of hearing the sound of his own overtures performed by the Austrian regimental bands. Wagner's first Venetian abode was in one of the Giustiniani palaces not far from Ca' Rezzonico; his last was the grand Palazzo Vendramin, now home to the Municipal Casino of the city. It was here on 13th February 1883 that he died of a heart attack, while visiting Venice with his second wife, Cosima, the daughter of Franz Liszt.

Although much myth has grown up around Wagner's memory, and although facts about him are distorted by prejudice, as his friends relate and as these two extracts, taken from his letters, show, there was an often endearing normality to his life—requesting supplies of snuff from his friends, or showing his concern for animals (among the last things he wrote was an open letter pleading against vivisection). In the final extract quoted below, which is taken from his autobiography, Mein Leben, Wagner beautifully evokes the melancholy of the songs of the Venice gondoliers—something which had also struck his compa-

triot Goethe (see p. 92), 70 years earlier. From the very beginning of his acquaintance with Venice, Wagner sensed the pervading sadness of the city: here it took on a peculiarly musical aspect.

Letters (1835–65)
Richard Wagner

To Ernst Benedikt Kietz, an artist and friend with whom Wagner corresponded for nearly 30 years.

Venice, 18th October, 1858

O Kietz!

…I'm living in Venice for the present, in the greatest seclusion so that I too can recover and collect myself—I'm already succeeding. I had my grand piano sent here and am working again. I'm living very nicely on the Grand Canal and am altogether charmed by the place. Having no plans, I'll wait to see how things will shape up. There you have everything I can tell you about myself without going into impossible details.

You could do me a big favor if you would get me some snuff. Can you afford to lay out the money for 3 pounds (1½ kilograms)? I can't send money to France in a letter, and no one will give me a draft for 12 to 14 francs. If you find it possible, please buy me 2 pounds of the regular and 1 pound of the special kind *à la divette*. Send them via Marseille, *par mer*. Since one can bring in only very little for personal use, I'll ask you please to send it in two packages. One to me: Canal Grande, Palazzo Giustiniani, Campiello Squillini [sic., for Campiello degli Squelini], No. 3228; the other one to Herr *Karl Ritter*, Sottoportico die [sic.] S. Zaccaria, No. 4691.

And now, behave yourself. I'll soon come to Paris again. Let me hear from you before then and remain faithful to your

R.W.

To Wilhemine Planer, Wagner's first wife, an actress. Theirs was a tumultuous marriage, and the couple frequently lived apart, though they kept in contact by letter up until Minna's death in 1866.

Venice, 20th November, 1858

My dear Minna!

…Karl [Ritter] has found a photograph which also shows my palace [enclosed]. You will see my three windows and the bay window quite distinctly. Watch it sometimes, and I'll be looking out of it.

—Today, on St. Mark's Square, a man again offered me a beautiful little dog. Only with difficulty could I part from it, and already the idea occurred to me to ask Karl to take it along for you. But it would sadden me too much to cause the good faithful Fips grief through such an addition to the family: certainly he would grieve if he were to get a successor in the house. As far as I'm concerned, I miss a little dog very much; and if for any reason I had believed or feared that I would not be coming back to you in the near future, I would have bought the little fellow for myself today. But you can see from that, dear Minna, how definitely I hope and how firmly I assume that I'll be with you again beginning next summer; *for that very reason* I'm not getting a dog so that Fips won't be unhappy.

I have nothing more to say to you today except that my recovery has been progressing rapidly. I'm in a really excellent mood for composing, and therefore I'm taking as good care of myself as I can in order to preserve it; for so much now depends on the completion of my work, in fact, the entire change in my existence. With *Tristan*—as you know—I return to Germany.

So take good care of yourself too; that's the most important thing with which you can make me happy. Pusinelli wrote to me giving me exact information about your illness and also an extraordinarily comforting consolation and real assurance, so that I see how understanding and sincerely concerned he is about your recovery. Be sure to follow his directions obediently! I entreat you!

And if you want to give me a present too, then get me—at Kressner's—*genuine Parisian* snuff, two pounds. And you could also give me a nice cigar case for small cigars, as I always smoke them. Karl will bring it along.

And now write soon; keep yourself quiet, have hope and confidence!

Accept a thousand greetings and congratulations from your

Richard

Karl is also bringing you the score of my *Rheingold*. You should keep it for the time being until I write you where you should send it.

Letters of Richard Wagner, *The Burrell Collection, edited by John N. Burk, Victor Gollancz Ltd., 1951*

Mein Leben (1870–80)
Richard Wagner

During one sleepless night, when I felt impelled to go out on to my balcony in the small hours, I heard for the first time the famous old song of the *gondolieri*. I seemed to hear the first call, in the stillness of the night, proceeding from the Rialto about a mile away like a rough lament, and answered in the same tone from a yet further distance in another direction. This melancholy dialogue, which was repeated at longer intervals, affected me so much that I could not fix the very simple musical component parts in my memory. But on a subsequent occasion another special experience revealed to me all the poetry of this simple song. As I was returning home late one night on the gloomy canal, the moon appeared suddenly and illuminated the marvellous palaces and the tall figure of my gondolier towering above the stern of the gondola, slowly moving his huge sweep. Suddenly he uttered a deep wail, not unlike the cry of an animal: the cry gradually gained in strength, and formed itself, after a long-drawn 'Oh!' into the simple musical exclamation 'Venezia!'. This was followed by other sounds of which I have no distinct recollection, as I was so much moved at the time. Such were the impressions that appeared to me the most characteristic of Venice during my stay there: they remained with me until the completion of the second act of *Tristan*, and possibly even suggested to me the long-drawn wail of the shepherd's horn at the beginning of the third act.

Mein Leben, *Richard Wagner, anonymous translation, London, 1911.*

WILLIAM WORDSWORTH

The great romantic poet William Wordsworth (1770–1850) spent most of his life in the picturesque Lake District in the north of England, with which his name is still so strongly associated. He only briefly visited Venice, in 1837, many years after he wrote the poem quoted below. In his youth he was an admirer of the 1790 revolution in France ('Bliss was it in that dawn to be alive', he later wrote), but by 1802, when he composed the poem below, he had witnessed the bloody consequences of that revolutionary idealism and was beginning to see the extinction of the old order in a more melancholy light.

Wordsworth rises far above the hackneyed descriptions of decadence and cruelty which were to characterise much 19th-century writing on Venice (scenes of hapless wretches being executed in St Mark's Square where moments before masked revellers had cavorted in the sunshine—see Samuel Rogers on p. 158). Instead he gives us this charming sonnet suffused with the bright, hazy light of one of J.M.W. Turner's Venetian watercolours.

On the Extinction of the Venetian Republic (1802)
William Wordsworth

Once did she hold the gorgeous East in fee;
And was the safeguard of the West: the worth
Of Venice did not fall below her birth,
Venice, the eldest Child of Liberty.
She was a maiden City, bright and free;
No guile seduced, no force could violate;
And, when she took unto herself a mate,
She must espouse the everlasting Sea.
And what if she had seen those glories fade,
Those titles vanish, and that strength decay;
Yet shall some tribute of regret be paid
When her long life hath reach'd its final day:
Men are we, and must grieve when even the Shade
Of that which once was great is pass'd away.

Poems in two Volumes, William Wordsworth, Longman, 1807.

SIR HENRY WOTTON & IZAAK WALTON

Curiosity, trade and diplomacy brought an increasing flow of Britons to Venice in the first half of the 17th century. The republic was still prosperous, and while her economic importance may have been on the wane (James Howell notes the impact of the changing trade routes as early as 1621; see p. 110), strategically she was as important as ever, having helped to defeat the ever-threatening Ottoman Empire at the naval battle of Lepanto in 1574. But it was not only against the East that she offered a bulwark for Europe, it was also against the perceived threat of papal ambition.

Sir Henry Wotton (1568–1639), poet and diplomat, first visited Venice as a spy for the Earl of Essex in 1595. When Essex was executed for treason by Queen Elizabeth I's government, he judged it wise to spend more time in Italy, assisting the Duke of Tuscany in warning the future James I of real or imagined popish plots against his life. Ten years later he was rewarded by James with a knighthood and the post of ambassador to Venice, a position he held on and off until 1624. As can be seen below, it was he who coined the phrase 'an ambassador is an honest man sent abroad to lie for his country', a witticism that briefly cost him his job. A friend of John Donne and a proficient poet himself, his Character of a Happy Life, *based on a Latin original, is given below.*

Izaak Walton (1593–1683) is best known for his book The Compleat Angler, *a lengthy essay on the joys of fishing, but he was also a friend of Wotton's and wrote his life. The extract below covers Wordsworth's arrival in Venice and the 'lying ambassadors' incident.*

The last extract is from a letter of Wotton's—1,000 are still in existence—informing his patron, the Duke of Salisbury, of Galileo's development of the new Dutch invention, the telescope, and the use of it to make some amazing astronomical discoveries.

The Character of a Happy Life (after Martial) (1612)
Sir Henry Wotton

How happy is he born and taught
That serveth not another's will;
Whose armour is his honest thought
And simple truth his utmost skill!
Whose passions not his masters are,
Whose soul is still prepared for death,
Not tied unto the world with care
Of public fame, or private breath;
Who envies none that chance doth raise
Or vice; Who never understood
How deepest wounds are given by praise;
Nor rules of state, but rules of good:
Who hath his life from rumours freed,
Whose conscience is his strong retreat;
Whose state can neither flatterers feed,
Nor ruin make accusers great;
Who God doth late and early pray
More of His grace than gifts to lend;
And entertains the harmless day
With a well-chosen book or friend;
—This man is freed from servile bands
Of hope to rise, or fear to fall;
Lord of himself, though not of lands;
And having nothing, yet hath all.

Reliquiae Wottonianae, Sir Henry Wotton, London, 1651.

Letters 1589–1611
Sir Henry Wotton

To the Earl of Salisbury

13th March 1610

...Now touching the occurrents of the present, I send herewith unto his Majesty the strangest piece of news (as I may justly call it) that he hath ever yet received from any part of the world; which is the annexed book [Galileo's *Sidereus Nuncius*] (come abroad this very day) of the Mathematical Professor at Padua, who by the help of an optical instrument (which both enlargeth and approximateth the object) invented first in Flanders, and bettered by himself, hath discovered four new planets rolling about the sphere of Jupiter, besides many other unknown fixed stars; likewise, the true cause of the *Via Lactea* [Milky Way], so long searched; and lastly, that the moon is not spherical, but endued with many prominences, and, which is of all the strangest, illuminated with the solar light by reflection from the body of the earth, as he seemeth to say [during an eclipse]. So as upon the whole subject he hath first overthrown all former astronomy—for we must have a new sphere to save the appearances—and next all astrology. For the virtue of these new planets must needs vary the judicial part, and why may there not yet be more? These things I have been bold thus to discourse unto your Lordship, whereof here all corners are full. And the author runneth a fortune to be either exceeding famous or exceeding ridiculous. By the next ship your Lordship shall receive from me one of the above-named instruments, as it is bettered by this man. Now to descend from those superior novelties to these below, which do more trouble the wise men of this place.

Our discourses continue with increase, rather than otherwise, touching the secret purpose, accorded between the French King and the Duke of Savoye, to assail the Dukedom of Milan; whereof I am unripe to render his Majesty any farther accompt. Always this is certain, that the French King hath, by his ambassador here, newly propounded unto this State a straiter colligation with him (as I take it) both defensively and offensively, enfolding some future great purpose *sotto parole tacite*. But I can assure his Majesty that the gravest here do neither trust the propositions of the French King, nor believe that he and Savoy can trust one another. And the thing which I much fear is this, that the very apprehension of the entering of foreign arms into Italy, will conjoin this State in better terms with the Pope; which a few days will discover.

The Life and Letters of Sir Henry Wotton, *Vol. 1, edited by Logan Pearsall Smith, Oxford University Press, 1907.*

'So much has been said and written, not only by learned men, but also by great scholars, that it appears to me there is nothing left to say.' So said Canon Pietro Casola about Venice in his *Pilgrimage to Jerusalem* (1494, translated by M. Margaret Newett, Manchester University Press, 1907). In this bibliography we do not include the titles of books from which our extracts have been taken, these are referenced at the end of each section of text. All we list below are a handful of recommended titles specifically about 'literary' Venice.

For a more detailed Venice reading list, Alta Macadam's *Blue Guide Venice* (8th edition) contains an extensive bibliography, which can also be found on the Blue Guides website (www. blueguides.com). And both J.G. Links's *Venice for Pleasure* (see p. 126) and Hugh Honour's *Companion Guide to Venice* (see p. 104) contain excellent lists with notes. Recent editions of both are still in print and available from the book trade as well as their publishers' websites (www.pallasathene.co.uk and www. companionguides.com).

- **In Venice and in the Veneto:**

- **with Henry James** *(edited by Rosella Mamoli Zorzi; published by Supernova, 2005);*
- **with Ezra Pound** *(by Rosella Mamoli Zorzi, John Gery, Massimo Bacigalupo, Stefano M. Casella; Supernova, 2007);*
- **with Lord Byron** *(by Gregory Dowling; Supernova, 2008).*

These literary walks through Venice are published in association with the University of Venice.

- **Poetry of Place:**
Venice *(edited by Hetty Meyric Hughes, Eland, 2006). An anthology of poetry.*

- **Paradise of Cities** *(by John Julius Norwich, Doubleday Books, 2003). Venice's 19th-century history traced through profiles of her famous visitors, mainly writers, including Byron, Ruskin, James and Browning.*

- **The Charm of Venice** *(by Alfred H. Hyatt, Chatto & Windus, 1912). An earlier anthology of writing on Venice with a large and varied number of short extracts.*

Numbers in bold denote major references. Numbers in italics denote text references to the maps on pp. 8–17.

contd. from p. 4

Photo editor: Hadley Kincade

Photographs courtesy of: © 2009 Jupiterimages Corporation
pp. 26, 29, 45, 86, 113, 119, 143, 186; the University of
Texas Libraries, The University of Texas at Austin pp. 33, 67,
89; Wikimedia Commons pp. 174, 206; The Bridgeman Art
Library p. 177; Dr Hans-Peter Haack p. 128; The Library of
Congress p. 191; © The Solomon R. Guggenheim Foundation,
Photo Archivio CameraphotoEpoche, Gift of Cassa di
Risparmio di Venezia, 2005 p. 94.

The patterned background on the cover is based on the end-
papers used in the 1891 illustrated edition of W.D. Howells's
Venetian Life

ISBN 978-1-905131-32-7

Printed in Hungary by Dürer Nyomda Kft., Gyula

Contributors

Charles Freeman: Pietro Bembo; Gasparo Contarini;
Petrarch; Marcel Proust; Marin Sanudo
Thomas Howells: Bernard Berenson; Elizabeth Barrett
Browning; Robert Browning; Lord Byron; Casanova; Wilkie
Collins; Thomas Coryate; Charles Dickens; Hugh A.
Douglas; Albrecht Dürer; John Evelyn; Peggy Guggenheim;
L.P. Hartley; Hugh Honour; James Howell; William Dean
Howells; J.G. Links; Jan Morris; John Julius Norwich; Ezra
Pound; Anthony Powell; Samuel Rogers; J.J. Rousseau;
Effie Ruskin; John Ruskin; Mark Twain; Giorgio Vasari;
William Wordsworth; Preface; Some Literary Landmarks;
Bibliography
Nigel McGilchrist: Baron Corvo; George Eliot; Goethe;
Henry James; Thomas Mann; William Shakespeare; Richard
Wagner